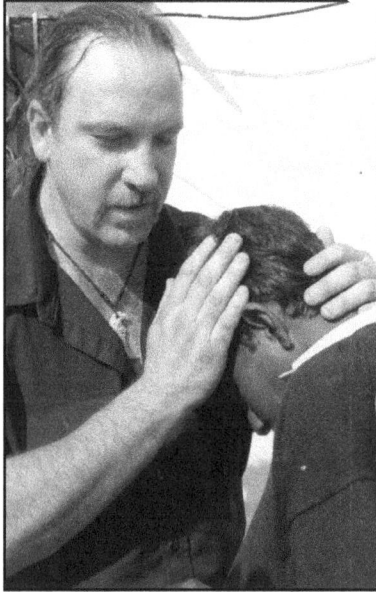

To the Saints of Christ of whom

I have the honor of serving with in

the

Glorious labor of our Lord's kingdom.

Reflections

on

Intercession

Standing Tall on Our Knees

CONTENTS

Introduction

After the release of my last book "The Most Excellent Way", I envisioned writing a follow-up book talking about my most wonderful journey with God and all the amazing things I have seen Him do thus far in my journey. However, it seemed to me that I needed to narrow that margin down a bit so that I could spend less time writing and more time doing. It is my goal to spread the gospel and encourage the saints. Therefore, in keeping in line with that goal, I will start with a topic and see where it goes. I will attempt to keep the rabbit trails to a minimum and stay focused on this books topic – Intercessory Prayer.

Now, before we get too far ahead, I feel it is important to let you know that this is not a text book. It is a look back at my journey in prayer and some events and how they unfolded through prayer. It probably will not make a good study guide. Perhaps it will be a good tool for small group discussion. Maybe even a useful tool in a larger setting. Regardless of where you may find it suitable for the benefit of encouragement and strengthening of the bride of Christ, remember that it is not an exhaustive look at intercessory prayer. Nor is it the final chapter of my intercessory experiences. For that to be so, I would have to be on my last breath, and really, I can't write all this in one breath. What it is, are things I have learned in my labor as an intercessor. You will read amazing things God has done in front of me and others through prayer. You will come to know some of the hardships and struggles of intercession, and the sacrifices that were made along the way. It's a journey that we will take together in this book. Through taking this journey with me, it is my deepest desire that you become stronger, first in your relationship with Jesus, and second, that you become stronger in your own prayer life.

With all this said, let us begin our journey together...

Chapter 1
Early Prayer

A lot of times in the Christian world, we like to compartmentalize skill sets and callings. We like to say neat definitive things like this person is an intercessor, that person is a prayer warrior, he over there is a Pastor, she beside you is a profitess, etc. While I will attempt to stay away from an in-depth look at calling and skill-set, I will set before you this true statement: **All followers of Jesus have a calling, and therefore, a skill-set for ones calling which would include intercession.**

We are all intercessors to one degree or another. Intercession is by definition, the act of interposing oneself into a situation on behalf of another.

One of the great men of prayer that I have tried to learn from has a book that he reads and re-reads. He once recommended it to me, so I went to the Bible book store to look for it. They didn't have that particular book so I picked up another book in Intercessory prayer. There was a lot of good stuff in that book. The one thing in particular that stood out to me was a definition that read something to the following effect: Intercession is to intercede through prayer on behalf of another person or situation for the purpose of bringing about God's will, or for the purpose of enforcing the victory at Calvary. After reading many books on effective prayer, and many years in the "prayer trenches" of intercession; I would whole-heartedly agree with this definition.

Intercession is not the passive, sometimes lazy, placing of a situation or person before God and ending it with a non-committed "not my will but your will be done" clause (we will speak more about that later).

Intercession is in fact an outpouring of one's heart, and sometimes body, and even life for that which one is interceding for. We will see more about this as we go on through some of my experiences. For now, it will be easiest for you, the reader, to just accept that I am right.

Let us touch back about the books I mentioned but failed to share the title of. It is in no way to say that I disapprove or disagree with these books, it is just that their names slip my memory and when I set out to search for them in my library, I find that they have become lost amidst the many books I have. With that said, I encourage you to read, read, read! Read how others have prayed effectively. Read about the results of their prayers. Be inspired to reach for new heights in your prayer life. In fact, as you read this book, understand that I am nobody special. God doesn't answer my prayers because I am better then you or at some great level of advancement. As if I have some special power that you as a believer do not have. On the contrary, I am just a man who is in love with his redeemer. I have come to realize that God wants to reveal himself to me and through me. The same as He wants to do with you. He wants to reveal himself to you, and through you. As you read, put it into practice. Do not just build up head knowledge of what someone else experienced. Build up a testimony of Gods manifest power displayed in your life through prayer. Be courageous and bold. Don't be arrogant in your boldness, and don't be foolish in it either. But, do not be weak minded and half-hearted in your prayers. Understand, you are a representative of the most high God. Act accordingly. As you read we will talk more about authority and our exercising of it. So many times I hear true believers speaking scripture out of context, twisting it to serve their purposes. Sometimes, taking on a robe of utter arrogance. As if God were their servant instead of us being his servant. Or even abusing the authority we have been given. Such grievous acts of ungodliness! Don't fall into these traps. Become knowledgeable of the heart and desire of God. Give thought to every word you speak, especially in intercession. For it is in intercession that you are truly acting as an agent of God. Therefore, be a competent and honorable agent.

Imagine if you will a sheriff. He is an elected official empowered with authority. However, his authority is not for him to use however he chooses. He is granted that authority to protect and serve the people. He has boundaries to the limits of his authority. He has the authority to kick in the door to your home. If he kicks in that door without serving not only the technicalities of the law, but also fulfilling the intent of the law; than he is abusing his authority. Too many Christians exercise their authority that God has given us, in an abusive form. When we are not fulfilling Gods desire in the exercising of our authoritative powers, we are abusing our authority.

While I am heading down this path: Allow me to touch on something else I frequently run into that brings great sorrow to my spirit. That is men and women that seek to quote another's prayer verbatim because it worked for that other person. All too often I hear wonderful people of Christendom say specific words because that is what so and so prayed and it worked. Think about that for a moment. God has not given us a "spell book" of magical incantations that if spoken in the correct fashion a great result will come about. Prayer is not correct phrases and specific sentence structure. Prayer is about connecting your heart and Gods heart. The words we use are our language. They need to be the verbalization of your heart being communicated to God. They are not "ten easy sayings to manipulate God". If you're looking for the effective spells and incantations book you are in the wrong family. Our family serves the God of all glory who desires our willing truthful heart and for us to see our willing truthful heart. Remember, God knows our heart. All too often, we are the ones who do not know our heart.

This is partly why it is important for us to speak our hearts in prayer and not just think them.

I had nobody to tell me these things in the beginning. I sure couldn't put most of this stuff into words at that time. I just prayed. Now for starters, it is probably important to remind you that I did not come to the loving embrace of Jesus in a revival service or any kind of church service for that matter; meaning that I was not raised in church. That is not to say that that is a bad way in which to meet him. That is just not the way I came to meet Jesus. If you read my first book "The Most Excellent Way" you will remember that. No, I learned to pray by reading the Bible and praying the way they did (the men and women in the Bible). That does not mean that I used their words. Instead, I used their style if you will. It would have never occurred to me to use their words. First, I was not them, and second; our situations were different, if not in general, at least in the specifics. It wasn't what they prayed so much as how they prayed. They prayed aloud. They prayed as if God were there in real person. Not some distant deity that stood unseen. And they prayed from their heart.

Their words were an outpouring of what was in their heart. That is how I would pray.

Let me give you a bit of a visual to help you understand. Actually, I teach and recommend this to everyone I talk to at any length about effective prayer. I would set up two chairs. One was for me. The other one was for Jesus. Now his was always the better of the two. I would invite him to sit with me. I would then begin to pour out my heart to Jesus. All the time talking to the chair as if He were there. Now I tend to get really animated when I get wound up in prayer. So it does not take long before I am up and out of my chair walking around. Understand prayer is a heartfelt conversation with the creator of everything. It is not some reverent utterance of words quietly released into the air with the hopes that it will eventually drift into the presence of the Holy God who is distant and removed from his subjects of which he created. NO! It is an outpouring of your heart and being to a personal and intimately close God who loves you and cares for every element of your life. Yes it is true that we must be reverent when we speak to Him, for his station as Holy and perfect, creator, giver of life; demands reverence. But it is also true that He desires honesty, love and fellowship from us, and with us.

Mind you, I do understand that some people say they have effective prayer lives, even effective intercessory lives while only having "quiet" prayer time. I won't debate that with you if you are one of those types' of people. However, please hear what I have to say on this point.

Think of prayer as a dance. Imagine if you will your old high school dance. I realize for some of us this may bring back bad memories, but look past those and indulge me. The school gymnasium with music playing; a few couples out on the dance floor engaged with one another. Some small groups of people gathered together laughing and talking. Then there are those sitting and standing along the outer perimeter. For those couples dancing together, there is something that is happening. It is more than just bonding. It is something that goes beyond just getting to know someone. Many first kisses happen there. Many beautiful memories result from that intimate time spent together. For our groups of people laughing and talking together, they can look back with fondness at times for those moments. However, those moments will never have the same positive deep impact for them as the close relationship of the couple dancing has. Now for those sitting and standing around the perimeter, they are there, but they are not really participants are they? They are more like observers waiting for something good to happen. Perhaps, occasionally on a good night, that special someone comes up and asks them for a dance and they step out and dance. Seldom does that happen. Maybe another side-liner finally screws up their courage to ask for a dance, typically not.

Here is the point. For those of you who pray actively, but never become expressive in your prayer (maybe not as much as me) you are like that group of people at the dance who are talking and laughing. There is benefit and reward for being at the dance. But, there will never be the intimate, passionate love that happens like those who leave the group and go one on one and dance with Jesus. Those of you who just give up the prayer that has no heart in it; no out pouring of what is inside you, you are like the ones sitting and standing around the perimeter. You will not truly get to experience the dance. Until you have danced with Jesus, you have NO idea what you are missing. This holds true for prayer as well as worship. The greatest dance partner you will ever have is the Lord of Glory. It doesn't matter if you know how to dance or not. He will lead. He will sweep you off of your feet and you will fall in love. As long as you hang on to your resistance, or your religious naivety, you will be at best, the people in the groups laughing. More than likely, however, you will find yourself as the ones sitting on the outside. You will be the ones missing the greatest romance you could ever dream of. It sometimes takes willpower to get off the sidelines and into the dance. But believe me, Jesus is not going to reject you, He has been longing to dance with you.

Something we really need to bear in mind here is worship. As you grow in prayer and intercession you will find that worship and prayer become intertwined. You will begin to see that one is at times a part of the other. At other times you may see that the two cannot be separated. Prayer is one form of worship, and worship is a form of prayer. Effective prayer cannot be far removed from worship and adoration of our Holy God. Neither can effective worship be far removed from prayer and intercession. Both are heartfelt expressions poured out before the God we love. Music, dance, flag waving, and other forms of expressive worship are conduits of connecting our heart with God's heart. I have seen and been a part of great feats of intercession that were Holy Spirit guided worship services. I have also experienced the most wonderful worship that was comprised solely of prayer. These two seemingly separate categories collide and become an indistinct avenue of the outpouring of one's heart.

When we get past the "I need" list of prayers we begin to enter the realm of intercession. Intercession is not about me, it is about others. It is the interposing of oneself into a situation on behalf of another person. It is selflessness in our heart and prayers. Remember, regardless of what you do in Gods kingdom labor, intercession will take your labor to a superior level.

Chapter 2

In The Name of

Jesus, Amen.

One of the early times that I got to witness the power of God through prayer was when I wanted to have a concert for Jesus. Allow me to qualify the following events: I imagine that others were praying also, but I never heard them and they have never told me they were.

So, as I was saying...

I had rented the city park stage for a Saturday. I also invited a band to come and play. The pastor of the church I was attending had a concessions trailer and brought that down. He was going to pass out free drinks and hot dogs. In addition, a man I knew that road motorcycles and went to the church agreed to lead a motorcycle "run" or procession for those of you who are unfamiliar with the term "bike run". This was going to be a great time worshipping the Lord!

As Saturday dawned, there became a flaw in the plan. It was raining! It didn't really faze me. God has all authority over the weather; therefore, the rain was not going to be a problem. The pastor showed up. The band called and asked if

I still wanted them to come, I said sure! The man on the motorcycle came out, and I will never forget our conversation.

He said "We should cancel this; the weather man said it is going to rain like this all day."

"But God knows more about the weather then he does" I said.

His response to my statement, "yes but, the weather man said it will be pouring down rain all day and no motorcycles are going to show up."

I was dumbfounded. How could a believer take the word of the weatherman over Gods authority. I told him to do whatever he wanted and I walked back to the stage.

The band was just arriving in their big van and they couldn't unload their equipment until it stopped raining. What were we to do? I had spent money I didn't have to rent the park. This band was here by my invitation; the pastor had spent money on drinks and hot dogs. Nobody was going to show up in this rain. I could just cry.

I did what every sane, Jesus loving, Bible believing Christian would do; I prayed.

"O Lord my God," I began as I knelt in the center of the covered stage. "You gave me a vision of a multitude celebrating and worshipping you. And you know that I have done all this because I love you. We have come here to celebrate who you are because you are worth celebrating."

"Lord, you know that we cannot celebrate you here today in this rain. You are the God who can command the weather. At your word alone the storm clouds would flee. I ask you O Lord; send this rain away until we are through worshipping you here today. Thank you Jesus."

That was the end of my prayer. I got up and went back to the others and stated as a matter of fact, that God would move the storm.

I don't know what the others thought when I said this. Perhaps they reasoned that that is exactly what God would do. Maybe they thought the typical; God will do what God will do. Weather they thought I was sane or off my rocker I couldn't say. What I can say as I stood there is that I had not one small doubt that God would somehow make the rain stop.

As we stood there for those few seconds looking at the front corner of the covered stage. We could see the rise of the Tennessee mountain, or large hill (where I come from, that's what it would be) behind the stage. The entire sky was covered in clouds as the rain drops continued to fall to the ground.

Nobody spoke as we witnessed God display his might. It was as if a giant arm settled over the top of the large hill. As I looked, it was as if it was stretched from my right extending to my left. Suddenly in a sweeping motion the clouds began to move. They first parted, and then were swept out of the way. It was, in a moment, a clear blue sky. No more rain drops.

We worshipped for probably two hours that Saturday afternoon. We celebrated the King of creation. We danced, and we sang. We loved our God and rejoiced in His love for us. What an amazing Saturday that was. When the last piece of equipment was loaded back up in the van, the clouds rushed back in and the raindrops began, once again to fall earth-ward.

Praise God! For He is mighty and His voice commands the Heavens. The clouds shall obey him. The rain ceases at his word. The sun warms the Earth and all men, at the nod of his head. He and He alone command his creation with complete authority.

Let us pause here and seize some understanding as to what went on in regards to prayer and intercession.

First we need to understand that this was intercession. I interceded in an event or circumstance to bring about or birth, Gods desire. It was Gods desire for us to worship and praise him. One, he covets our praise of himself. And two, he is the one that gave me the vision of this celebration.

This is what an intercessor does. They birth Gods desire, or heart, from the spiritual realm to the physical realm. Or, they enforce the victory at Calvary. This, in all honesty is covered by the first statement.

The second thing to observe was that I didn't command God to do what needed to be done. He is not mine to command, rather, I am his to command. It is important to always remember our place. He may call me friend and son, but He is still GOD!

Third, I allowed God to determine the solution. I was not imposing my thoughts on what the solution should have looked like. I am reminded of Josephus writings on Moses, the Israelites, and the Red Sea experience. I will be brief in my paraphrase.

Basically, they came to the shores of the sea. They had the sea before them, mountains to the left and the right, and Pharaohs' army behind them. They had no weapons or skill in which to engage this army and defeat was certain. Moses cried out to God. Not in a desperate, I am afraid prayer, but in the calm, you are God prayer.

He said, "O God of Abraham, Isaac, and Jacob, you see the trouble we are in. We have gone where you commanded us. Now we have Pharaohs' army behind us, mountains to the left and the right, and the sea that lies before us. You surely did not bring your people out here to parish. O God, you could level these mountains that we could walk across them. You could part this sea that we may walk across on dry land.

You are the God who can lift us from the Earth and carry us in your hand to the safety of the other side. I ask you God to deliver your people from the hand of Pharaoh's army."

We all know what happened next; God displayed his wisdom and mighty power. He decided on the course of action.

Let God be God. Let us be His servant.

Another thing you may notice, I didn't end my prayer with "In the name of Jesus, Amen". Let us take an opportunity here to talk about why that is.

Most Christian people that I have met end their prayers with "in Jesus name, Amen"; or something similar. I am not sure where this comes from originally, but I assume it has come from scripture where Jesus says that our father in heaven will give us anything we ask for in his name (the name of Jesus – John 16:23). It is not in the literal name of Jesus that he is referring to here. It is the nature and character of which he is that is being spoken of. If I ask God our father for something that is contrary to his nature, but I ask for it *in the name of Jesus*, meaning the literal name, does this make God bound to grant that request to me? That would be a resounding NO! That is the only impossibility for God. He cannot act contrary to who he is. If he did, he would no longer be perfect, but instead become a liar. God cannot lie, nor can he act contrary to who he is. Therefore, it is not in the literal term of the name that is being spoken of here. It is in fact, the character and very nature of the person that is being spoken of. Let us look at the scripture again in this way; *I tell you the truth my father will give you whatever you ask in my name* (the nature and character of Jesus, son of God, part of the triune being of God).[NIV. parentheses added by me]

You may wonder why I felt it necessary to drive into this point. This is not a new and strange theology I am speaking of here. Although for some it may seem as though it is. It is crucial for the man or woman of God to have a firm understanding of scripture, especially when we are laboring in our prayers. If I am commanding, declaring, ordering, or travailing, it is important to understand that *in the name of Jesus* is not some catch all incantation. Instead, the very name sums up the boundaries of my authority. I grow so weary of Christians who obviously love the Lord. Who try very hard to walk in the manifest power that the Lord bestows upon his children and followers. And yet, treat His name as if it were a magic key that if affixed to the end of any request or statement , no matter how contrary to the will and nature of Christ it may be, will make it all happen anyway. Jesus, the true son of God; the glorious one to whom all authority has been given; He who is unsurpassed in strength, wisdom, and power; this same Jesus cannot act contrary to who he is. With that said, we can continue on in this line of understanding. God is not going to do contrary to what He has determined to do. He is not going to pause midstream and say "O, well, Mickey (or put in your own name) has declared in my sons name that this or that won't happen, therefore, I will change my mind and not do it." That would be contrary to what God has already ordained and again, that would make him out to be a liar, and THAT CANNOT BE!!! So for the man or woman of meaningful effective prayer, that puts us in an awkward place sometimes. None of this is to say that we do not use his name in prayer and intercession. We just have to remember that his name is not some magic word. The name of Jesus is the Holy one of heaven, the one who sits in all authority, and it is under his authority we operate, therefore, we must not exceed those boundaries. Remember, when we operate outside of the authority we are subjugated to, then we are misrepresenting the one we represent; in this case King Jesus. That can spell disaster for those you are ministering to. You see, as you intercede into a person's life, or a group of people's lives, you impact their lives. If you are releasing a word to them, and you are outside the right kingdom boundaries, you can do a lot of damage in their life. As you mature in the kingdom, the weightier your word becomes in its impact into a person's life. The greater responsibility you have in their life. By speaking wrong kingdom words into their life, especially kingdom promises and life direction, you can set them up for disaster. It is imperative that we seek out what God wants to do in the situation. So, just what does God want us to do? How do I find that out?

These are very good concerns and vital pieces of information that one must know to pray effectively. Before I answer these questions, let us first address another beautiful piece of scripture that is abused and assaulted by well-meaning yet naive followers of our wonderful Jesus. Matthew 26:39 (NIV) ..."*My Father, if it is possible, may this cup be taken from me. Yet not as my will, but as you will.*"

I hear over and over people praying very powerful sounding prayers, prayers that are filled with confidence and assurance, prayers that give great hope. Then suddenly they are dashed to pieces because they add the tag-line "not my will but yours be done".

WHAT!

You mean you have no idea what God wants in this situation? Then why on Earth did you start praying like that? I will especially hear it in healing prayers a lot. You come out of the gate boldly declaring healing and restoration, and even blessings, than you make a statement like that?

I am not sure about you, but I do not want the man or woman that has no clue what God wants in my life to pray over me or my circumstances. I want someone who knows what God wants and speaks it with confidence.

If I am going to someone for prayer, I am expecting results! If you're gonna pray that I am healed, then I expect to be healed, PERIOD. Don't throw some catch-all, just in case I'm wrong 'cause I have no idea what God wants for you, clause. Holy bejeebers batman, I find NO comfort in that. On the contrary, if it is not going to go the way I hope, I want someone confident in their prayer over me and not wishy-washy. I need God's truth in my life. I figure it's a given that you don't want to see me suffer, but what I really need is God's truth. I don't want to get pumped up just to find out you were wrong. However, if you're wrong it is okay, you are human and subject to mistakes, no matter how hard you strive for accuracy. But you have to take responsibility for your words. Not giving yourself a fire escape, by shifting the responsibility of your words onto God.

Matthew 26:39 is not Jesus saying that he is not sure what God the Father wants him to do. It is Jesus saying, Father this is hard. I would rather there was a different way; everything in this body is repulsed by this which must be done. If there is any other way then for me to be separated from you for even an instant then I would rather do that. BUT, I know there isn't. I submit myself to what must be done, I submit myself to your will.

It is a statement of willful submission, not confusion. Let's not make it say something it doesn't say by miss-using the words of our Lord. To get back to our questions: Just what does God want us to do? How do I find that out?

Ask God what he wants. Ask him how you should pray. It will not always be the way you want it to go, but it will be the right way. Because it will be Gods way and His way is always right. We are a son or a daughter of the most high God. Our words are representing Him.

Let me share an incident that brought brokenness to my heart because my desire was to pray one way, but God directed me to pray an entirely different way.

There was this young woman I knew. She was just out of her teens and had her whole life ahead of her. On her way to work, or maybe home from work, I don't really remember which now. Anyway, she was driving down a road at night. It was raining when she lost control of her car and hit a tree. She was rushed to the hospital in critical condition. When I got there she was in a coma and, if she lived, she would probably be a vegetable. Her outcome was bleak. The family asked me to go and pray for her. I was more than willing to oblige. I will never forget seeing her lying there hooked up to all those machines. My heart broke immediately upon seeing her. I walked over and laid my hands upon her. I knew for her healing, it was going to be a great visible manifestation of Gods wonderful power. That meant for me that it was "let's get serious and pray time". I started my prayer the normal way. I poured my heart out to God. I told Him what I saw. Cried out for what I wanted to happen. Then when I got myself out of the way, I simply said "Lord, how should I pray?" In my mind, I just meant, should I labor in this prayer for her healing? Would it be a total healing? Should I stand up boldly and command her to wake up? How do you want me to pray God? See. That is the thing. I can have all the feelings and desires I want to, but in the end, I am here to represent God in the situation. Regardless of what Mickey wants, my place is to pray what God wants. I would have loved to boldly command her to wake up and be completely healed. How cool would that be? Bleak outcome predicted by all the hospital staff and suddenly she stands up pulling all the wires and tubes from herself and walks out to her waiting family! Ta-da!

But that is not what Jesus had in mind for her.   There is a reason my prayers get answered. I pray what God wants. Not what Mickey wants. I gave my life to Him. It is not mine anymore. That is not to say that I do not tell God what I desire and want. That is not to say I don't give Him my wish list. But when the rubber hits the road, it is my place to pray His Will and not mine. The only way I can pray His will is to ask him. Then listen to what He says about it.

On this night, my heart was about to break. He said pray peace and for her to take comfort in Him and for her to let go. She was to die. It was her time. Her family wouldn't see the joy in it. Many people would come and pray life into her, hoping that she would be returned to us. She was a believer. So it wasn't death for her, it was a passing from here to the place of our hope. Go tell that to the weeping family grasping any thread of hope they could get ahold of. When I was finished praying, and got myself squared away, I stopped back in to see the family. They asked how it went and I simply told them that everything was going to be okay. She loved Jesus and He loved her.

After a few days or so, maybe longer, I don't really remember. She began to show signs of improvement. She was transferred to some kind of care facility. Shortly after her transfer she went on to be with Jesus.

This was a case of "Not my will, but your will be done." If there was any other way, I wanted God to do that instead. But, I willfully submitted myself to Gods will and not my own. That is who we are to be. When occasions have arisen where I have tried to simply pray my will and not seek out Gods will in a situation, I have usually found myself looking foolish in the outcome. You see intercession is not about imposing what I think or hope God wants into a situation. It is about bringing about through prayer Gods plan. It is okay to say God I would like it to be this way or that way, but, it is not okay to pray contrary to Gods way. If you do, you will find yourself out on a limb without Gods hand to catch you when you fall.

.....

These were my early days in prayer. Days when my intercession was limited only to specific events; one time of prayer. Not several, not days or even years, just one prayer. But really, that is what it always is; just one prayer at a time. I think upon reflection, that what changes isn't the prayer so much as the understanding of the scope of how that specific instance ties into a much larger picture.

In those days I would have never called myself an intercessor. I don't think at that time I even herd the term. It wasn't for several more years before I heard that term and used it. I wasn't familiar with the term prayer warrior either at this time. I prayed because I could. I sought out what God wanted me to pray because I was His and my responsibility was to pray what He wanted to happen. It just made good sense to me. If you love God and you believe God knows what is best; if you work for God and expect results; you pray what He wants. What sense does it make to pray what God doesn't want? That is what the enemy does. He works against God. How many good intentioned Christians are actively working against God? We say "God knows everything." Or "we are laboring for the purposes of God", yet we never bother asking Him what He wants. It just really doesn't add up to me.

I have found that my most effective prayers are when I start out with "Lord, how should I pray in this situation?" One of the most important skills in effective prayer is to be a good listener – to GOD!

The level of ones sensitivity to "hear" God is proportionate to ones practice at it. In other words, the more you practice the better you will become. It is also related to the integrity of your walk. That is something most of us do not want to hear. Believe me, I understand. It can be hard to make godly choices when your body or mind is focused on what it can't have. But when we walk in the places that are contrary to Gods ways, they take us further from God. Our purity and our righteousness are extremely important factors in our prayer life. If you want to witness the power of God flowing through you, you will have to keep a clean vessel for him to use. God don't get dirty. I cannot stress enough the importance of our purity. Hearing believers say things like "I am just a poor old sinner" is such a terrible thing. We cannot use our humanity as an excuse to sin. We have to understand that we are new creatures. We may not be perfect; we may find that every day we are faced with many temptations and struggles, but we are striving for godliness in our lives. It is of the utmost importance that we determinedly push forward in our pure walk. Be quick to repent of sinful behavior in our life. To not confront the sin in our own life, sweeping it under the rug and blaming it on the fact that I am a poor sinner saved by grace is a terrible thing. To have effective ministry in general, more specifically effective intercession demands that we do all we can to remove the obstacles that lay between us and God. How can we serve Gods kingdom plans and minister to the people he wants us to minister to when we allow our life to be littered with roadblocks?

Again, let me say this: We are all intercessors. We may intercede for different things and have different areas of responsibility, but we all intercede. It drives me up a wall to hear people say "Well, I'm not called to be an intercessor." That is ridicules! We are all called to advance the kingdom of God, to effect change in this world for the purposes of God. We are all called to pray for the sick, the hungry, the impoverished, fatherless, governments, leaders, our fellow believers, etc. I think you get the point. We all have responsibilities that require us to exercise effective prayer. I could give you Webster's definition of the term Intercession and Intercessor, but I won't. All you need to know is that it is a legal term that basically means to be in the middle of something. That is what all of us who are believers do; we get into the middle of something. We get between man and Satan. We get between God and people, God and His desire, and people and their situations. The real question is who are you fighting for; God or something else?

That brings me to another point I would like to touch on briefly before I get too far along. Whose side are you on?

Once as I was leading an intercessory prayer group in a church, that very issue came up. The situation was difficult. The church body needed to move spiritually into a different place. The Pastor needed to go there first as the leader of the body, and then the body needed to follow. There was a great potential for a church split during this time. If the Pastor stepped into this place, many people would become uncomfortable. When people get uncomfortable in church, they begin to grumble. If they find no satisfaction there they usually start to work towards forcing their satisfaction. Often that ends in a church split.

Our task was to, through prayer, move the entire body into the place it needed to go. While discussing the potential of what might happen in this delicate situation, one of our prayer team members said "Well, our job is to back up our Pastor." While I know they meant well, that was not our job. That is never our job. Neither should it ever be yours. Our side is always Gods side, if they are on Gods side then fine. If they are not on Gods side then, pray for them, but don't get on their side. If you do that, you will find yourself on the wrong side. Who can stand against God?

.....

Allow me to share another example of 'standing on Gods side'. Years ago, I had the privilege to launch a type of crusade to help to bring unity among our area churches. I had no idea what I was doing, but I saw clearly what needed to happen. As a part of this effort I had sent letters out to all of our area churches inviting them to a free meeting to share how we can make a team effort to reach the lost in our community. At that time there were approximately 211 Christian churches in our area. I sent letters to all of them. Guess how many responded? No really guess. ONE! I was surprised and disappointed at the time in the response. However, looking back and seeing the ridicules control issues that we, as churches have; I should not have been the least bit surprised. We are either too busy with our own agendas or we have a "we don't work with those kind of people" mentality. How sad that we are not one unified body UNDER Christ. We are for Christ, but not always under him. Anyway, this will become a rabbit trail, so I will steer back to where I was going.

I found out later that this church that responded was in a desperate way. They were dying and grasping at any small hope to see life come into their church. It was headed by a Pastoral Husband and Wife. At this point, I had a wonderful group of lovers of Jesus that were with me. We canvased the neighborhoods surrounding this little church inviting everyone to our crusade. We tried, without success, to contact some of the larger churches located near this little one to create a cooperative effort. It was my first experience with the hostile territoriality of some churches.

Our little band of loyal lovers of Jesus canvased the neighborhood with fliers and prayers. We went to every house we could walk to. Our crusade ended up having maybe thirty people at it. Considering the church only had about seven members at this time, I guess this could be considered a success. I found it as a sign of a sickness that consumes many churches today.

Anyway, for me this relationship with this particular church was more than just a crusade.

It was also about the assisting a church body to step into their purpose from God.

First I had to know who these people were. What was their purpose? How could I best serve them by serving God? These answers came from prayer. Heartfelt, focused, intimate relationship with Jesus prayer. In addition to these questions, I needed to know from Jesus how He wanted me to implement the things he instructed me about.

Long story short, my place was not to share with the church body or even the pastoral team what God instructed me in. It was to help keep them focused on learning those truths from God himself and then confirming it to them when they received that word. In their specific case, the vision of this particular church body was so vastly different from what their traditional view of church looked like that they needed the confirmation that what they heard God speaking to them was correct.

During these several months, there was an increasing excitement among the body and the leadership for this wonderful plan God was laying out before them. There were some obstacles that their particular denominational governing, by nature, required us to overcome. God is always good for making the impossible possible! Also, during this time, as would be expected, the leadership team and I built a very close relationship. Then came a day of crossroads.

It was a Sunday evening. I was taken completely by surprise. The Husband came to me to talk and informed me that he wanted to disciple me into becoming ordained through their denomination. Furthermore, he did this in front of the small congregation. My heart broke. I had come that night to say my good-byes. My time with them had come to an end. My work with them was done for now. I tried to politely decline the offer. I stood and spoke encouragement over them on this journey they were setting out on with Jesus. That's when the Husband (the husband and wife were co-pastors) became angry and said that he didn't want me to leave and that I being discipled by him was the right thing to do. I told him that that was not why I was here. I tried to remind him of when we first met and the things we heard from God along the way. Then I reminded him of the destiny of their beautiful congregation and that if I stayed, it would take away from that destiny God had for them. Remember this, WE ARE ON GODS SIDE. He became very angry and said he didn't want what god wanted, he wanted me to stay. He didn't quite yell, but he was very loud and very adamant about it. I told him not to say that. I remember pleading with him not to reject what God wanted for their church. He wouldn't budge on his opinion. I left with a broken heart. I felt as if all that labor was just flushed down the drain. I wept all the way home. The real shocker came with-in a week. The doors of that little church closed. Their denomination governance cut all funding to that church for no understandable reason. Today, that building belongs to some business that seems to be doing quite well there.

The bottom line is this: We are always on Gods side. We belong to him. We are not on our side. We are not on our churches side. We are not on our pastor's side. We are only on Gods side. Sometimes we may find that to be very heart breaking. As was the case with that little church that I dearly loved.

Chapter 3

Our Foundation

"Though I speak in the tongues of men and of angels, but have not love. Then I am nothing more than a resounding gong or a clanging symbol. If I have the gift of prophecy and can fathom all mysteries and all knowledge, and if I have faith that can move mountains, but I have not love, I am nothing. Though I give all I possess to the poor and surrender my body to the flames, but I have not love, than I gain nothing." (I COR 13 NIV)

Salvation aside, prayer is probably the greatest gift given to us from God. I am not talking about that religious obligatory prayer. Not the formalized grouping of words that sounds moving to the listening audience. Nor am I talking about that creative stringing together of words, Bible verses, and pleas, designed to try and motivate God to do what we want. No, I am talking about that beautiful communing with God our Father and creator. That pouring out of one's deep heart and allowing God to fill it back up with something different than what was there. God sent his true son to step out of heaven and into this world to restore us to himself. He then dispatched His Holy Spirit to direct us and help us along our journey. But He also gave us a means to communicate with him! That says something right there; God wants to be an active participant in our individual lives. How great is that!

.....

This church I once went to when I first became a lover of Jesus had scheduled a revival service. I was new to this church stuff so I had a few questions. My biggest question was: How do we schedule when God will show up? Do we book Him for revivals? Although I was asking a sarcastic question, the planning of a revival didn't make a whole lot of sense to me. If a revival was a move of God: Decided in time, place, and circumstance by God, how then could we plan it? It just didn't make a lot of sense to me. I can't say it does today either. I chalk it up to one of those religious expressions we use. Anyway, as our revival service was drawing near, we began meeting every week for prayer. I discovered something about these people. They could pray when they wanted to! The same group of people who typically just said religious sounding prayers came alive in these prayer meetings. It was fantastic. For some of them, I imagine that they prayed this way at home. However this was the first time that I had heard many of them pray outside of the church building. To be a part of a group of people pouring their hearts out before God; WOW! Of course, after the revival service, they reverted right back to the way they used to pray. How sad. However, while the prayer time lasted, it did something inside of me. It stoked up an already burning fire. I couldn't get enough. I needed daily time set aside specifically for this revival. By golly gee Whittaker (what-ever that means), if we were going to have a revival then we needed God to show up. And if He didn't show up it surely wasn't going to be because Mickey wasn't praying for it. So I decided that every day during my lunch time I would go to the church sanctuary and pray for this revival. What an awesome plan. Or so I thought. There were some great times of prayer there. Some were even better than the group prayer times. Not because of any doings or lack of on their part. No, this time became more personal and intimate. Understand, at this time in my walk, my day typically consisted of about an hour of private prayer time in the morning and an hour or more of private prayer time in the evening before bed. I was no stranger to intimate heartfelt prayer to God. This was the first time that I began to focus prayer on a single subject. The first time I began to labor in prayer for something that required more than a single prayer. I didn't realize it at the time, but I was beginning to step into a new level of prayer.

Something I have come to learn in prayer is that God will deal with your junk at the same time as you are praying for other people or circumstances. God is easily capable of multi-tasking like that. You may find yourself shocked to learn what God wants to deal with in your life in the midst of intercession. Here lies another key to effective prayer - **Work with God**. If God has something He wants to deal with in your personal box of junk while you are in the middle of interceding, than let Him deal with it. Don't table it and say that you will work on that latter. No, if God is bringing it up now, then deal with it now. Never allow it to become an obstacle in your relationship with God. It will build in size until it is the only thing to focus on. If God is bringing it up now, it is because He wants to deal with it now.

I hope you got that because it is going to become a huge factor in my life in just a few more sentences. Now, pay attention.

...So there I was on my knees in the middle of the sanctuary. I am crying out to God that we desperately need Him to manifest himself in this revival so that these people would see His greatness and become in love with him. The words pour out of my mouth, "I will do whatever it takes for you to manifest yourself in this revival service". Pretty awesome thing to say in my prayer, isn't it? Isn't it awesome how we usually do not truly realize the impact of deals we make with God? I do not know about you, but sometimes this stuff just comes out of my mouth never really thinking what it may end up looking like.

I will never forget this moment. I concluded my time in prayer at the church and needed to get back to work. I stood up, turned around and headed for the sanctuary doors at the front of the church. I walked down the aisle wore out from the praying but filled with such delightful joy from being so near to God! Life just couldn't get bad! As my hand reached out to take ahold of the door handle, God spoke. It was just a gentle sound in my spirit. Not the resounding sound of His audible voice that shook every fiber and cell in my body with its resonating power. But even his whisper can seize your attention. In that moment his words brought me to a stand-still. He said "I want you to tell your wife about your affair." I was frozen. My vow to God echoed in my ears. It was still swirling in my mind. From my own lips came a deal "I will do whatever it takes for you to manifest yourself in this revival service."

I sure didn't see this one coming.

Now, before you get to judgmental here let me put this into its rightful perspective. Before I met God, I lived a very different life. As for my wife and I, we had a relatively open relationship. Promiscuity was a part of our lifestyle. But we did have some ground rules. You could be with another partner sexually with each other's consent. We were no stranger to this lifestyle, although it wasn't an everyday occurrence. Thing was, there was a woman that I went to see without my wife's knowledge. Therefore, by our own rules, that was an affair. Now this had happened years earlier. In fact it was before I had met this beautiful savior and fallen in love with Him and His ways. Now I live by his standards (or at least I strive for it always).

"Why was this important now?" This was all that kept going through my mind. As you can imagine, my day from that point forward drug on slowly.

I can still remember driving home from work and telling God how cool it would be if I went home told my wife and in turn she told me that she forgave me and in fact, she confessed to an affair also. What a juvenile way to hope for an outcome. I knew that wouldn't be the case, but for some reason I sure thought it would make it easier on me. When I got home I sat in my chair and she was sitting in hers. We had a small lamp table between the two chairs that faced the television in our little home in east Tennessee. There the two of us sat watching television. Well, in all honesty, there she sat watching television. I was trapped in a time zone where every moment seemed to drag on for hours. Where the conversation between God and I repeated over and over. It echoed through my head so loud that I am shocked that she never heard it. I tried to focus on my reading. I was reading the Bible. It was awful! It seemed as though every passage of scripture I read was nothing more than a continuation of the conversation God and I had earlier. I couldn't stand it anymore. I turned to her and said that I needed to talk with her in the bedroom.

We went into our room and sat on the bed. I explained to her about my prayer time earlier that day. I reasoned that if she knew that part of it, that she would have to forgive me and everything would be okay. I would have come clean. She would forgive me, we would become closer together, and God would really do something great among that church body. See, it all works out!

When I admitted my infidelity, it was as though the entire planet stopped for a moment. She hit me, yelled, a lot, and then gave me the what-for. Then she proceeded to tell me that she wasn't sure that she was going to stay or not. That went well.

So here I was, trying to honor what God told me to do and now my marriage was in ruins. As you could imagine, I slept alone that night. The next morning came and I drug myself off to work. My day was not looking real bright. I kept crying out to God. Why would he have me admit something that happened long before I met him, which would destroy my marriage? This appeared to be a terrible turn of events. I was confused and left to feel as though I had been belly punched.

As you can imagine, driving home from work that evening was terrible. I expected to find the house abandoned. My wife and my son, nowhere to be seen. Thankfully, that is not what happened. In fact, I could have never guessed what would happen. I got home and my wife was waiting there. As I come through the door she said that we needed to talk. So, again, we stepped into the bedroom. As a side note here. Let me just say that the bedroom of the husband and wife should NEVER be used as the argument place.

...Okay, back to where I was at.

My wife and I sat down on the bed and she began to talk. Her first words were, "I owe you an apology." Ah, I thought, she and God had

had a talk and now she was going to forgive me and everything would work out fine. Her next words caught me a bit by surprise. She said, "I had an affair before that. I was angry at you and thought that you might have cheated on me, so I went to my friend's house and had an affair with an old boyfriend." Talk about flabbergasted! I wasn't sure what to say at first. But then I realized that the most important thing was that she knew that I forgave her. So I said it. "I forgive you." No leverage to gain her forgiveness. No using it as a bargaining tool. She trusted me with this, and I knew first-hand how important it was to hear those words and know them to be true. Eventually she did give me forgiveness.

The point of this is, sometimes God will want to deal with your junk while dealing with something else. I was praying for God's out pouring over a certain body of believers. Basically God used it as a means to open an infected sore in my marital relationship. It came down to this, did I really mean the promise I made with my lips and was I willing to trust Him.

Imagine with me for a moment... Instead of dealing with the affair, which really was really a part of my old life, and not the new me; it came from the dead man who was now transformed and redeemed. Was it really important that that was dealt with? After all, it was in the past, and that past was not who either of us were today. The answer is a resounding YES! These are all deep issues of the heart and God wants to address these issues, each in its time, so that we may grow and mature, becoming a true reflection of who He is. Even though we are redeemed, there are still places of wounds and death that remain in us. God will address each of these places in their turn. Spiritual growth and hence, intercession, will become handicapped if we do not continue to be healed and have life spoken into places of death. Also, as in my above example from my own life, it wasn't just about me. My wife, and therefore my marriage had a hidden secret of death exposed to the Holy light of truth, and from there healing can begin.

Intercession is our means of warfare. Weather it is intercession through prayer or intercession through activity, it is our mode of battle. To become proficient in our walk with Christ; in our activity of intercession; we must grow and mature as believers. Part of growing and maturing is dealing with the junk.

I have tried to live in relationship with Jesus and not allow him to deal with the dirty spots in my life. You can only go so far and then you hit what seems like a spiritual wall. It is as if God is saying "That's fine, but until we deal with this, you cannot come through this door." Remember, He holds the key.

Not all things are as Earth shaking as my previous example. There are many things in our lives that will have to be dealt with along our beautiful journey. Perhaps a little phrase that we say or an expression we commonly use. Maybe a bias we have that we never really realized we had or never took the time to think about. Maybe a habit we have that God says "Today child, because I love you, I want to point out something in your life I want you to be aware of and change." How much he must love us to be so aware of every intimate detail of our life and to deal with each of those that are not right! Sometimes we may get irritated, as my son does with me, but really, would you change it? Would you trade it for anything else? The patient,

unyielding, attentive, make you feel like you –
are – the – apple - of – his - eye love! I wouldn't
trade it for everything in the world. It can be
scary and very unsettling at times when God sets
something of mine on the table he wants to work
on. It can be something simple that makes me
burst out laughing at the realization that I do it.
Sometimes it is something serious. It can
sometimes be so difficult and hard. But he
walks right there beside me. As him and I sit
and talk, he listens to me. How do I know this?
Because of the results that follow.

Let me share a simple example in my life. I
have never really worn a seatbelt unless I was
drunk, road racing, or saw a police officer. Not
an uncommon thing. I think a very large portion
of Americans behave in this same manner.
Although they may not road race or drink. For
the record, I do not drink alcohol any more, just
in case you were wondering. Anyway, why would
God put something as little as this up on the
table? SUBMISSION! O that dreaded word! One
day I was driving down the road, and God gently
and quietly asked me why I didn't have my
seatbelt on. I never really thought about it
before that time. I wore it when I was behaving

recklessly or it seemed to be dangerous, but I was never nessisceraliary against them. God began to point out that we, in this case –I was willfully not submitting to an established law. That is rebellion. There was nothing in this seatbelt law that was contrary to God, yet I was not submitting to it. O man! I laughed so hard. What could I say? I buckled up. He also pointed out the speed thing. I still find myself having difficulty with that one, especially on my motorcycle. One motorcycle in particular that I have. It runs best at between 80 and 85. Nothing like a well running bike on an open road..... Ah well, let me not stray off in that direction here.

Let us just set everything about us on the table before God. Let us deal with each and everything he points out. Rejoice in it. Strive for it. Every issue becomes a step closer to that beautiful place of greater relationship with Jesus. It is such a terrible thing to dread it. Some of the blessings of walking this path are closer relationship with the one whose love for you surpasses everything else; it also establishes you as more capable of standing in the Holy place God has given to you to stand in.

Chapter 4

Emotions

Do you remember when you first met Jesus? When you first accepted him into your life? Do you remember the rapturous love you had when you submitted yourself to him? How about the "I will do anything for you" love you had in that day.

If you do not remember that, then I pity you. That first love is some of the most beautiful love you will ever know. For some of you all those wonderful emotions may still be coursing through your body. If that is the case, then I envy you; but only in a small way. The early love and the emotions with it are so wonderful. The newness and freshness of it all. It is to me, like the first blooms of spring at my place in North-East Tennessee. There is a newness in the air. Leaves are budding out, and the air has changed from the wintery cold, then suddenly! Suddenly, a colorful fragrant flower appears, and not just one, but soon, dozens of them. The anticipation and excitement that builds in me as I wait for this bloom is almost overwhelming. My roses and flower garden I plant and nurture. Winter has not been my friend in a long, long time.

Injuries and a weird cold allergy that seems to come and go at will make winter a less then joyous season for me. Spring to me is the promise of relief from pain. It is also a great ray of hope. Winter at my place is sometimes very difficult. You get up from a cozy bed to stoke up a fire. Get my son up for school. Just about the time the house gets good and warm you turn down the fire to head out the door for the day. Darkness comes just as you get home so for an out of doors person, it becomes frustrating. About an hour after your home the house is warmed back up enough that it is comfortable. Than its fix dinner, get clean, say prayers, tuck in my son, read a little, and then go to bed myself. The only advantage for me in Tennessee winters, is I get to get plenty of rest. When spring comes, it is like being paroled from a prison. I get all excited. Lots of work begins to happen around my place. I check all my plants and see who made it through the winter. I look to see which flower will be the first to bloom. I watch it bud out. Then painfully slow it begins to unfold. Then comes that amazing morning when POW! It bursts fourth! I try to take a picture of it every year. To me it is the most wonderful morning. When we first met this beautiful savior called Jesus, it is new and fresh: a releasing from a cold prison. There is excitement and lots of animation. For some, sadly, from that point on it is a slow dying out of a great light. It breaks my heart to even think of that. For others, from this point forward it can be an exhilarating and sometimes difficult journey. I have been the latter of these two. The thing is, we cannot stay in the first place with Jesus. That beautiful young love is good and one must experience it, but there is so much more. This is a journey. There is so much Jesus wants to show us. He wants us to grow and learn and become radiant! He wants the world to see his great love through us. We become his love letter to mankind. Instead of written on pages it becomes written on our hearts, read in our actions, heard with our words. That first place is wonderful. Like the early days of a newborn. However, they cannot stay there it is not good for them. They must grow and mature. Likewise, we must grow and mature. There is much depth in the word of God that he wants to teach us. More than that, there is the application of his word. I think of it as taking a walk with Jesus. At times there will be difficulties and hardships. We will find suffering and heartbreak. There will be moments of overflowing joy and a happiness that causes us to stop the car and get out and dance on the side of the road. It is an amazing adventure with the one who created the universe! We can never ever experience the wonders that await us if we simply try to stay a baby. Or worse yet, if we allow fear or pride to stop us from taking the hand of the one who truly loves us and has nothing but the best for us in mind.

I love the firsts and the new with Jesus. He never ceases to completely blow my mind away. You don't usually get a text book or even a warning. It just suddenly happens and then you get to process it. As a new believer, I had an opportunity to travel to Romania on a mission trip. I had absolutely no idea what to expect. One of my early BAM moments in learning came on the streets of Bucharest. Bucharest is the capital city of Romania. I have no idea what the population is, but it is a lot. It has an old history and has been conquered in recent history by the Nazis and then the Communists. Today, Romania is again a sovereign nation. However it is one of the poorest if not the poorest in Europe. We had just spent about two weeks having an awesome experience with Jesus among the Romanian saints. We were on our way out of the country. One more night and we would be on a plane headed back to the United States. Walking down a main busy six lane wide road; cars everywhere going to and fro, zooming past us; my mind was a swirling mess of thoughts. We were on our way to a Kentucky Fried Chicken to get something to eat. As we neared a streetlamp pole, I turned my head to the right, something had caught my attention. There sitting on the side of the road, dressed in rags, was a woman. She had a kerchief on her head and she wore a tattered dress. She had a coat that had seen better days and thick torn and worn stockings. She was an older woman. She appeared to be old enough to be someone's mother and maybe even a grandmother. Her ankles were red and swollen. She wept in pain as she pan-handled for money. But it wasn't the obvious that struck me. No, instead it was far deeper. As I looked at her, it was like getting hammered into a wall. It took the wind out of me and nearly sent me to my knees. I looked at this woman, but I saw something more. For just a moment I saw the broken heart of Jesus over the city we had been working in-Slatina. In my journal I called her mamma Slatina. To get, even for a moment the impact of the greatness of the sorrow of our Lord for a whole city is overwhelming. I do not really have the words to correctly describe it. Imagine feeling all the pain for hundreds of thousands of oppressed and impoverished people all at once. It really is more than one can bear. Perhaps if more Christians got to get a glimpse of Gods broken heart for more people groups, we would become completely driven to bring the hope of Jesus Christ to these people.

Let me just say that even in this early BAM moment, I rejoiced in Jesus for it. Like an unexpected belly punch, it nearly brought me to my knees in the middle of a foreign city, leaving me in a bit of a daze and with a crushed heart. Yet, for all the harshness of it, I felt closer to God because of it. The more we can experience Gods heart for people, the closer we get to God. This can be painful and give a person a lot of sorrow to carry. But to truly intercede on the behalf of another person, you must carry at least some of their pain and suffering. Otherwise, you can only bring a request before God and not a heartfelt plea. One of the greatest tools and highest honors as an intercessor that we have is to truly feel another person's pain. In this we can share in Christ's sufferings. We get a glimpse of what he knows fully. With this glimpse we can set a heartfelt plea before God and not just words of sympathy.

In our growth from infancy to maturity, we will have many opportunities to feel another's pain. Sometimes this may come in the form of one person's pain and at other times it may become many peoples pain. Let me share a few examples.

Let me first share an example of an individual's suffering. Now, as a father, I find it very easy to feel my son's suffering. You know the suffering, the pain, and the sorrows and the anguish of those around us who we truly love, is sometimes easy to feel. But what about those you don't know so well. Or perhaps a complete stranger! To feel someone's suffering doesn't necessarily mean you understand it. Many times I have laid my hand on a person and I was flooded over by wave after wave of emotion crashing over me. Not just from women, but from men also. In fact, I think some of the strongest individual sharing of strong emotion has come from men. As a side note, for you wives who think your husband is a man without the capacity to be affected by things because of his outward expression, or lack there-of. You may be truly surprised to feel the depth of emotion he carries. Typically, as a man it is not in our culture, and sometimes our make-up to be expressive about our hearts. It is generally a taboo for a man to be too emotional. I don't think that is always a bad taboo either. A man is created to lead and be a warrior; to be a protector and a defender, especially of his family. Too much outward emotional expression undermines that duty and takes away from the security a woman and your children need to see in a man. Speaking as a former Marine; if you have a leader that is always blubbering and emotional, he becomes a hard man to follow into harm's way. You cannot feel confident in trusting his decisions. Regardless of how capable he is. On the other hand, a leader who is solid, decisive, and exudes self-confidence (even when he is not) is a man that we can follow into harm's way without hesitation. That is not to say that he cannot show emotion just that the emotion is not the fore-front of his make-up.

Wives don't look at your man and assume his lack of crying and pitying means he does not care or is unfazed. He may not know how to verbally express it, or may even think it just doesn't need expressed. What he needs from you, his help-mate is to know that he is human and his heart has depth. Help him express it by lovingly and gently drawing it out. All too often, he has it in his mind that if he expresses it you will think less of him and his ability to be strong. While in reality it is a part of his strength, he needs to know that you feel secure in him and trust him. By understanding that your seemingly stoic man does have a deep heart, and not embarrassing him because of it, yet still allowing him to share it with you in trust, you will strengthen your man by leaps and bounds. Okay, that is my free tip for you ladies out there.

...moving on...

Where was I? O yes, laying hands on a stranger or a person you really don't know well. You may not be able to express the flood of emotion you feel or perceive and that is okay. Most of the time, it is not necessary to tell them that you feel their pain. You're probably not there for that anyway. More than likely you do not even know what is going on in their life, or at least not the specifics. So don't worry about it. Just put words to what you feel as best as you can, then send them up to God. A good word picture is that you are lifting a burden off of them and setting it at the foot of the Lord for them. That is where the healing actually takes place anyway; at the foot of Jesus our King. One time in a church, I went up to a man whom I felt the need to pray for. Gently, I laid my hand on his back and instantly I was flooded with an ocean of sorrow. It was all I could do to speak. Some of the emotions I was familiar with, others came from things I could not identify with. What I did was begin to pray. I just began to share with Jesus what I was feeling as best as I could. Now, mind you, I share this aloud, just enough so that the person, in this case a man, I am praying for can hear what I am saying. This is important so that his (or her) spirit can confirm what is being said and prayed. Usually I have no idea what is going on in their life and I always have in the back of my head that voice saying "you're gonna make a fool of yourself." IGNORE that voice; that is not God. You can never ever measure the effectiveness of your prayer based on their reaction. At this point you are a conduit for "piping" their situation up to God and the conduit for God to bring what He wants to do into their situation. It is generally our desire that when we feel someone's pain to cry out for God to heal them. Understand, healing, or better yet solution to their problem will come. But as we mature in our intercession, we get to become more involved many times with the process of the healing or the solution. Back to the man I was praying for in my example. I was flooded with emotions. I had to take a moment to compose myself as this flood of emotion was not expected by me. I began to express to God what I was feeling, or sensing may be a better word to use here. I am honest in saying "God, I don't understand where this is coming from." I describe any images I have in detail. Never assigning meaning to the images unless the Holy Spirit gives me understanding of it. Mind you, I will always seek an understanding to the images but I don't rush it. I have found that for me at least, my intercession becomes very image based. I notice that as I speak in tongues I am flooded with images. It is as if there is a download of so much information that it cannot be expressed in words. It comes in pictures.

Remind me to come back to the tongues thing, we need to have a brief talk about that.

As I describe what I am sensing, I then ask God how He wants me to pray in this situation. Remember, we are on Gods side. This situation that this man, or anyone else for that matter, finds themselves in is an opportunity for God to be glorified. Does he want to bring healing, freedom, relief? I would say yes. Just remember that it may not always come the way you want it or the way they want it. Get out of the way and do it God's way. That is our purpose for interceding. If I just lay my hands on him and demand in the authority of Jesus that that man is healed, delivered from his strife, or whatever, and call it a day. I have acted immature and irresponsibly. My job, if you will, in walking in the authority and blessing of Jesus is for his kingdom not mine, His agenda, not theirs, His glory, no one else's. My immaturity or negligence may very well be robbing someone of a great blessing that God desires to pour out on them. So let us not be too hasty in worrying about the now problem. Instead, let us seek out and focus on the God solution. When we focus and pray into effect the God solution to a problem a few things happen. First and foremost, your prayer does not fall into the good intentioned well-meaning but unanswered prayer category. Second, the person you are praying for may not really believe that God will or is capable of solving their problem. It could be a case of "I hope God can". If they hear your prayer, then when God takes care of the problem just the way you prayed it; then guess who gets the glory! And guess how their faith grows. This goes for the believer and the unbeliever both. You pray what God wants to happen and amazing things begin to happen in people's lives. One time there were two women that came into the place that I worked. One was pregnant and the other was not. The non-pregnant woman appeared to be the mother of the other. The Holy Spirit just prompted me to go pray for the pregnant one. Now before we get too far ahead here let's understand the whole picture. I did not know either one of these women. To my knowledge this was the first time they had ever been there. The older of the two was probably my age or slightly younger while the new mommy to be was probably just into her twenties. If you can picture this...

I walked up to them as politely as I could and introduced myself to them. It helped that I had my staff t-shirt on that had my name and position clearly marked on it. For a six foot plus two hundred plus pound man to walk up and begin talking to two young women out of the blue can be an uncomfortable situation from the beginning. I went on to gently explain to them that if it was okay I would like to pray for the child as I felt as though God wanted me to. They looked at each other and said yes. I explained that I would lay my hand on the pregnant woman's belly as I prayed. They seemed a little uncomfortable but said it would be okay. I began to pray. As I did this, God showed me that it was a baby boy. Than He went on to give me a few words of encouragement to give to the mother to be. I told her that the Lord said not to be discouraged that there was no father in the child's life, do not feel overwhelmed by the feeling that you will have to assume the role of mother and father. Trust the Lord and he will send godly men into your son's life and they will become like father figures to him. Then the Lord began to give me words of destiny to speak into the mother for her soon to be son. When I was finished I handed them some tissues as they seemed to need them to dry the tears. And I thanked them for their time and I turned and left.

A little while later the mother of the daughter stopped me as I was walking past them. She asked how I knew it was a boy. I matter of factly said "God told me." And I went on my way. As I once again had to walk past them she stopped me again and asked the same question. I gave her the same answer. This time however, instead of letting me go she said "I know, but how did you know it was a boy? We just left the doctors and we are the only ones who know it is a boy. We haven't told anyone." I placed my hand on her hand and smiled as I gently said "God told me, that's why I went and prayed over you."

Imagine if I had just prayed some good health and protection prayer over the child. They would have smiled and thanked me and went on with their life. By praying what God wants into a situation it produces faith in those being prayed over and glory for God. Let us not forget that it also increases your faith.

. . . . .

It was just several days after hurricane Katrina had struck the shores of the Gulf coast. We were headed up to Pennsylvania to visit with my family for a few days. As we talked about the hurricane and all the troubles being reported in the media, we were suddenly overcome with a sense of urgency to pray. It was a two lane highway in West Virginia when this happened. I stopped the car and got out. I took just a couple short steps and hit my knees. I was overwhelmed with suffering. It was a tidal wave of pain and sorrow from so many people. All I could do was weep. I knew it was the people along the Gulf coast. All I could say was "Lord, if you want me to go now, tell me and I will turn the car around and go there straight away." There was no answer. I just prayed and prayed. After about two hours, I got in the car and we left. We continued on to Pennsylvania. The whole trip I could do nothing but think of how much I needed to return to Tennessee and make plans to head to Louisiana. Our homeward journey could not come soon enough. I had contemplated driving straight down from Pennsylvania through Tennessee into Louisiana. I didn't do that, mainly because I did not hear a clear word from God to do so. When I returned to Tennessee I expressed this incident to my mentor. I think it was the next day when it turned out that a relative of his was leading a disaster relief team down there and offered to let me go with them. Praise God! This one trip turned into several trips and a heart that remains even today for the people of lower 9th ward in New Orleans.

In the example of the man and in the example of the pregnant woman, I was flooded with emotions for a person. On the other hand, with the example of the Katrina disaster area, I was flooded with emotion from countless people. For an intercessor, emotions not your own are part of the package. Allow me to state this a little differently.

As a lover of Jesus we cannot help but sometimes feel the sorrow, the pain, and the emotions, of the people He loves. It is not bad for us to feel the weight of their emotion. In fact, this becomes a great tool to allow us to be powerful in our intercession. All too often I think we try to push these emotions away and respond unemotionally. Men tend to act this way more than women in my personal experience.

Although, I am of the opinion that a man who steps fully into intercession; releasing his inhibitions, tends to become a far more powerful intercessor than a woman. This is not because a woman has a lessor place then a man, but more because of the different places of authority between a man and a woman. A man was created to be the protectorate and the warrior. Intercession is typically a place of warfare. Unfortunately, in our culture and most of the cultures I have had the honor of visiting with; men commonly shirk their responsibility and therefore their ability. Women usually carry the load in that department. There seems to be some kind of false written rule that says it is unmanly to be an intercessor. As a gender we seem to treat it with a second class look. When in reality, it is the most powerful weapon in our arsenal, giving us an unparalleled ability to crush the enemy with mighty blows. I am not talking about some boxing event going twelve rounds, I am talking about a knock out in the first round as soon as the bell goes off. We are talking a lightning strike verses a cattle prod. Men need to really embrace this.

Chapter 5

A county-wide prayer and the act of intercession

While I would argue that all of us as believers are called to be intercessors both in prayer and in deed, there are also different realms of authority. I will not claim to have a full grasp on this, but I do understand that if you are working outside of your authority, you will be in trouble. Think of your realm of authority as the area you can effectively work in while God has your back. If you step outside of your authority, then God doesn't have your back in that place. You open yourself up to all kinds of problems.

I am of the belief that each of us has the opportunity to expand our realms of authority, but not by our own power. If we ask for it, then in due time, I believe Jesus will give it to us. You seem to have to be grown into the place to deal with the realm of authority you have. At times, God seems to give a special dispensation of authoritative powers to someone. This would seem to be the exception to the general rule that you must be raised up to the realm you are to operate in. I hope that makes sense to you. So, for the most part don't pick on something spiritual that is bigger than you are, you just might get your butt kicked! Do you think David had a chance against Goliath without God? How about the three young men in the furnace or Moses and the Hebrews coming out of Egypt? If you go poking your nose into a fight not yours, your nose might just get broken.

Let me share a little bit about a county God has had me interceding for, for many years. I know the end game because that is what he told me up front. How we will get there and what battles will be fought along the way, I don't know. I can say it has been interesting. Allow me to point out a couple things before we get going on this part. First, I know that I am not the first to carry a place of intercession over this county. Second, I am very sure that there are others out there battling and interceding for this very same county. Are we all battling in the same battles? I don't think so. I know there have been times when we have been in the same battle together without meeting, but generally I think we are each fighting along different lines of attack coordinated by God for the same victory. What I am certain of is my territory if you will, here in these United States of America. That is my county in which I live. The seasons of my activity seem to ebb and flow. Sometimes I am worn out by the constant state of prayer, at other times it seems as though I have little to do. It wasn't always this way. But honestly I cannot remember a time when I knew Jesus and did not have authority over this county. Perhaps it is wrong of me to say that I have authority over this county. Instead I should rephrase that so you do not get the wrong impression. It is not really the county I have authority over so much as the ongoing and upcoming spiritual war here. The physical boundaries of this section of the "front" for me seem to be defined by the boundaries of the county. It began with an evening in prayer before the Lord, as every good thing should begin.

I had gotten home from work probably three hours previous. I had done some honey-do chores and eaten dinner. After tucking my very young son into bed, I went out to my garden of prayer. This was my normal routine in those days. I would go out and pour my heart out to God there. I would give him my problems. Ask questions, make requests, and generally hang out with the King of kings. How cool is that.

It was in that time that God placed in my heart a burning to see revival come to my county. It is kind of hard to explain. It was far more than a desire, it was more like an "I'm gonna die if this don't happen kind of thing." At that time I began the Jehovah Nissi Campaign. I was pumped up! I sent out letters to all the churches. Prayed constantly for my county; tried to start a home Bible study –fellowship of sorts, inviting neighbors that didn't go to church. I had a couple dedicated believer's come alongside and together we prayer walked so many areas. Outwardly, it was an utter failure. The lessons I learned through it were gigantic building blocks for what was to come and is still in the process of coming. There were things about the church of today that my naive new Christian self-did not know or even suspect that went on. I did not realize the territorialness of many of our churches, nor the lack of unity under the common banner of Christ we have. The most shocking revelation was the total lack of genuine love for people in our own community! How shocking to a man that read the Bible and thought we were supposed to believe EVERTHING in it! Obviously I say that with complete sarcasm. I was outraged at the establishment we call the church here. Just for the record, since then I have come to love her in a way I am not sure I can truly express. Not that those horrid rotting death cloths are not still attached to her, just that in the midst of all the outward festering disease is a beautiful and brilliant diamond just waiting to glow. But let us return to where I was then.

I knew a revival was going to come to this county because God told me so. Furthermore I met two different people who confirmed this to me without even knowing it. One was a man who I had met only once. He shared with me how God had told him that North-East Tennessee was going to have a revival. My heart leaped for joy! Next came in a men's class. I was at my home church at the time. It was a Sunday evening men's discipleship class. We had a special guest teacher, a Pastor from a church in a nearby town. He actually used to be a part of that congregation many years ago, but at that time I didn't know that. At one point, and I forget exactly how it came about, his son was speaking. Now he was young by comparison to me. Probably 15 years my junior I am guessing. But there was something that glowed about him.

Something that filled a person's heart with Joy just to be near him, and when he spoke about God, it drew you in to a mesmerizing lull. He had that same something his father had. It was beautiful and I wanted it too.

.....Rabbit trail.....

You know, in this delightful walk of being a lover of Jesus, I am privileged to meet some of the most wonderful people that have ever existed in all of humanity. Most of who will probably never be appreciated by mankind for who they are. They have a glow about them that comes from being near to the Lord. It radiates off of them, at times to a degree that almost hurts because you become so conscious of your own sinfulness. Yet it is not some condemning, finger-pointing, holier than thou, religious superiority. Instead it is the beauty of love, of peace, and of joy. It is magnificent in its splendor even though it is fading. It is only received and sustained by being in the very presence of the most high God! O, how warm and pleasing it is. How much more pleasing it is when you experience it in first person and not just the fading aroma from another.

....Back to where I was....

He was sitting there sharing a vision God had given him. He said he saw two hands come down from heaven in the air. They were cupped and in them they were filled with water. No water dripped from them and it was all stored up in them. Then those hands opened and the water flowed out and poured out over the entire Tennessee valley area. From up in Virginia through East Tennessee and down into Georgia. It was an outpouring of God over this whole area.

Now I couldn't see all that he apparently could see, but I could see over this county. What I saw was just one small part of a much larger picture. I was pumped up! Jesus R-O-C-K-S!!!!

But what do I do? How does all this work? Is there something specific I should be doing? Like usual I did what I knew to do and waited on God. I prayed all the time for revival to come. In fact I am still praying for that, many years later. I know it is coming, but I would have never imagined then that it would be years away! I thought it was just around the corner. To this day I do not know the specific time it will happen. I do know this; it is on its way. It is coming and if you don't want to get caught up in the flood from heaven, you better grab your gear and run, because it's a coming! God has spoken to me, showed me things and overwhelmed my heart concerning this county I live in. One time, not to long after that, I was working for a guy who was building a house. God overwhelmed my spirit with these words "Dry bones arise". It was a good thing I was the first person to the jobsite. In fact I was about thirty minutes early. Had anyone showed up while I was... praying, they would have probably called the law on me, or at least an ambulance.

I stepped out of my truck to pray. I was so energized I couldn't sit still. It was a cool early winter morning in North-East Tennessee. The ground was frozen, I could see my breath, but it wasn't yet really cold. To get here you turned off the main road onto the driveway. Up a long strait grade that brought you to the top of a rolling hill, then you veered a little to the left as you continued on through what used to be an old farm pasture. Off in the distance a large barn was nestled in a pocket in the middle of this former pasture. It was being converted into a house. The first floor was simply a garage, but upstairs was being converted into a beautiful two story home.

I stood outside the door of my Chevy truck. As I looked out over the frosty pasture, I began to see a sight I never dreamed of. Overlaid in the pasture I could see skeletons and rusty weaponry and armor. It seemed to be buried but it wasn't in the physical, it was like seeing a movie being projected onto the ground in front of me. Then I was filled with powerful words. I began commanding in a loud voice "Rise up mighty warriors!" "Your day of resting is over! Rise up, gather up your swords!" In this movie like vision I could see them getting up and shaking the dust off of themselves. I saw them reaching for their swords and as I commanded they began reaching for each item of armor and shield that I called for.

Sounds pretty wild huh! Yeah, well you should have been in my shoes. There was an entire battalion of warriors there. Rising up from the ground where they lay as if dead. They gathered up sword and shield and began to move around as if they were alive. Before long I was on my knees worshipping God. My hands stretched to the heavens, my lips shouting praise. I lost all track of time. When suddenly I tuned back into this world, I had no idea where the warriors went. I was exhausted, spent, on my knees in a state of praise. WOW! That is really all I can say. I had just called some sleeping warriors up from all over this county. Something was happening and I didn't understand it, but it was wonderful.

It was right around this time that God began to speak into me a vision for a church that is one of several that is strategically raised up to help usher in what God wants to do in this county. I will speak more on that in the next chapter. All by itself it is a wealth of intercessory learning.

God later spoke to me as I looked at a map of our county and told me to look at it as if it were Israel. It didn't make much sense to me until He said to turn it just so. "See the river", he said, "It is positioned much like the Jordan." I reached for my map in the back of my Bible. Turning to the maps of the twelve tribes and their territory, I began to see my county in a different way. I took my county map and drew out each of the tribal lands over top of it. From here I began to pray over different areas of the county. I remained like this for quite some time. Several times I went to churches that God would send me to. I would visit there a little, usually in the evening service. I went to all kinds of different denominations, learning about the body. Much of what I saw was sadness. Most of the body of Christ seemed to be caught up in bondage. Religion had replaced the church. It wasn't all sad though, I met some wonderful and beautiful believers that wore the fragrance of Jesus on them. Many who I talked with wanted more, but didn't know how to get there. So many churches talked of the things we should be doing, yet more often than not, they did very little of what they talked about. Some even brought me to tears as they were so steeped and shackled up in their religion that they completely rejected anything of Christ's heart. As sad as it often was, there are many days when I long to travel around and meet with my brothers and sisters again. The joy when I meet one wearing the fragrance of Jesus.

Once I went to a small church. I usually do not dress up a lot to go to church. On this particular Sunday evening, I was wearing blue jeans, a t-shirt, and a leather vest with my Christian club colors on (that is the patch on your back some people who ride motorcycles wear that tells people who you belong to. In this case it was "Hard Core Disciples of Jesus"). I went in and sat down about half way back on the left side facing the pulpit. I had taken off my bandana, but my long hair was pulled back in a neat pony tail and held together by several pony tail holders. I was on my motorcycle and this was my traditional wear. It was a pleasant enough service. We sang a couple hymns from a red hymnal to the sound of an upright piano. After about three songs the preacher stepped up and began to preach. They were rather traditional so they used only the King James Bible. It was understandable considering the deep roots of the Bible belt. Men wore denim coveralls, woman wore full length skirts. We all sat in long wooden hard-backed pews. I seem to remember that there was an older woman sitting beside me and a father and teenage son sitting in front of me. When service was over, I shook as many hands as were willing to take mine. I wasn't offended, I knew that for most of these fine people I was a little different and therefore they tended to be a little cautious. My surprise came as I went to leave the sanctuary. Like a lot of old churches, centered on the back wall is the main entrance/exit. The deacons and the Pastor lined up and shook everyone's hand as they left. I also shook all their hands, the pastor being nearest the door and therefore the last hand you shook. He took my hand and thanked me for coming. He then, as politely as he could, handed me a set of papers and suggested that I read their by-laws before coming back! I was flabbergasted! I had never experienced that before. I was more insulted in that moment than when another Preacher had called me Satan! I stepped outside and down the four or five steps of this little country church and began to question God why he would send me to a place like this. I said to God that I didn't believe that I would ever come back here. Suddenly that older woman I was sitting beside in the church came up to me. She gave me the warmest hug I had had in a long time. She said "Thank you for coming here tonight." I told her thank you and said that because of her I will return to that church to visit. You know, one person can make such a difference. But that wasn't all. Several weeks later I ran into a young man. I didn't recognize him at first, but he recognized me. He asked if I was the guy that came and visited his church one night. He told me where he went to church at and I said yes I had. He said "You know, my dad and I talked about you all that night. You could just feel the spirit of God all over you. I wanted to turn around but I didn't want to be rude."

Praise God for that church. I love his people. They are a jewel. Sometimes you have to look beyond the outside, but inside, they are a jewel. I have had many experiences similar to that one. None exactly like it and each one different. The religious are cold and sometimes brutal. They kill people and rob them of joy and freedom and hope. They pirate their blessings and forbid them from dancing with the lover of their soul, yet in the midst of this, you find brethren; men and woman who are in love with Jesus. It is so refreshing. A room full of Christians but not many Christ followers.

Usually, with few exceptions God gave me a word of destiny for each church I attended. If it wasn't a word of destiny, it was a prophetic word. On rare occasions, like the previous church I mentioned, there was nothing of the sort. Now when I say destiny, I am not talking about where you are headed if you stay on this path, I am talking about the purpose a body has in Christ. It is surprising to see how many church bodies have no idea what they are there for except to meet on Sundays and maybe even Wednesdays and learn Bible stuff. Pot luck dinners, the occasional picnic, homecoming and a revival service and vacation Bible school seem to be all there is. One would think it was a social club and all too often that is all it is. When it was a prophetic word, it is almost always delivered in a positive encouraging way. It is rare and with great caution that I deliver a "woe to you" word.

.....Yes, time for a side-bar.

The profit has control over his or her mouth. It is with rare and very infrequent times that one must interrupt a service to present a prophetic word. Be sensitive to the order of things in the gathering you are at. Be submissive to the leadership of the church house you are in. You may be a mouth piece of God, but you are not God and there is leadership in the house representing God. Even if they are doing it incorrectly or disobediently they are still the representation of Gods authority over those people. Your submissiveness is not for them, but for the office they hold and the God who appointed that office. Never forget your place. If you are a "Woe unto you" profit, I would suggest that you consider your words carefully. While it is true that the prophetic word of God is sometimes for correction, it is also direction, encouragement, and the building up of the saints, not the tearing down. The profit is not above the people, we are not better than the rest of the saints. Do not set yourself in some lofty position as if you are greater than those around you. I either ask for permission to speak to the congregation or wait for the floor to be opened for someone such as myself to speak. The Pastor and his leadership team represent the God authority in that house; it is never your right to supersede it. They answer to God for their choices. If you find yourself about to declare the judgment of God over a people or situation, than I suggest you consider carefully each word that comes from your mouth.

.....End of side-bar.

One church I was at, God told me it was a house of prayer. The prayers prayed from this body had a special and powerful anointing. As I attended that church for a short while, I used every opportunity to encourage them to be a people of prayer. I spoke several prophetic words over them concerning this and several words of destiny about this. There were many, as there usually is, that never quite get it. At this particular church the Pastor was included among those who seemed to hear my words as if they were a different language. There were a few however, that would make your heart swell to hear them pray. They may not understand the scope of their prayers (although I think some have and even one did at that time), they would pray and you could almost feel the Earth move. That may sound like an exaggeration but it is not. I have the honor of praying with some of these people even today, several years later.

Another church God sent me too was again different than any other I had previously been to. In this one there was a Pastor who was very knowledgeable in scripture. Unfortunately he seemed to be very controlling. He always maintained control over every aspect of his congregation. This eventually put me in an awkward place. God showed me how he was taking the blessings that God was pouring out over the people and locking them up (I am speaking spiritually here). He would than dispense the blessings at his pleasure. It was as if the blessings could come from God, as long as they flowed through his hand to get to you. Talk about pride and self-importance! WOW! This was a delicate word. How am I to deliver this word, along with many other prophetic words for this congregation in general, and do it in a positive way? I contemplated this for a while before God. Eventually I wrote it all down neatly. I went to the Pastor one on one and spoke the word to him. Instead of saying "you" are hording the blessings of the people, I simply said the blessings from God are being horded by one of authority in this house. I then gave him the same words written out and asked if he would deliver them to the body. He agreed to do so. A part of this word said for the blessings to be allowed to flow freely or the people will be removed to receive their blessings from a different fountain. Nothing changed there and within a year all but just a tiny handful of the people had gone and begun to attend other churches.

Why am I sharing these stories of these couple churches? Simple, to demonstrate that intercession is not just a prayer, it is an action also. In my illustrations, I am sharing about my intercession into the churches in an area that the Lord has given me authority over. Let us move the example to something else. Pretend that you have begun to have a serious burning in your spirit for your local school system. The welfare of the students, the influences of the changing educational system. Maybe the lack of godliness or the acceptance and even sometimes the mandatory participation in ungodly life choices. The act of praying may be only one of the tools you have at your disposal. Consider running for the school board! Imagine the intercession you can make then. Talk about moving to the next level. God used Ester to intercede in the affairs of an entire kingdom. Sure God set the stage, but ultimately Ester had to "screw up" her courage and go and see the king. Imagine if he had not extended the scepter. She would have been very probably doomed to death. Likewise for us, God sets the stage, but we to must "screw up" our courage and seize the moment God has given us. Of course, also like Ester, seizing the opportunity God has given us is by faith; we never know how things are going to go until we take hold of it. Why do you think the most frequent advice God gave Joshua was, not to be afraid!

There are many times when prayer is the only practical way you can intercede. When that is the case PRAY! When it is not the case, prayer and action go hand in hand.

Chapter 6

Tongues, spirits, demons, and really strange things

For some of you this may get a bit uncomfortable. That's okay; we all need a bit of stretching now and then. If you have read my last book "The Most Excellent Way" or have at least read this one up to this point, you will know that there have been some seemingly strange things occur in my walk with Jesus. If, however, you just opened this book up to this page to start reading, may I suggest you back up to page one. This is probably not the chapter to start reading in.

You may have noted that previously I stated that when I speak in tongues I am flooded with a stream of images. As if I was receiving a download from heaven. It is a really difficult thing for me to describe in words or any other way. I didn't always speak in tongues. Actually I wasn't really a believer. I wasn't one who argued against such a thing, but I did believe that there was a reasonable explanation to it. Turns out there is, just not one I expected. First I should define what I mean when I say to speak in tongues. I have heard many arguments and debates over this very thing. Great theologians have debated this for many, many years. I have read word studies of the Greek and the Hebrew on it. Read articles and listened to many sermons about it. I knew people personally who claim to have this gift and when I would listen to them it sounded like rubbish. My general opinion was that in the context that most Christians today used it, it was false and untrue. Instead of presenting the arguments for both sides in this book, I will simply convey my experiences. Since I am the one writing this book, I get to do that.

The first time speaking in tongues became an issue was when I was interceding for a Church of God. I was a relatively young Christian, but I had already witnessed God do many great things through my hands and my prayers. The Pastor asked if I had been filled with the Holy Ghost? I told him I didn't understand what he was asking and could he please explain what he meant? He went on to tell me that when I was filled with the Holy Ghost, I would be able to speak in tongues and then be able to do all kinds of miracles. Since miracles were evident in my walk with Jesus, I simply replied that I was not the way he described it. This wasn't the first time I had been given a definition that if you were filled with the indwelling power of Jesus Christ then it would be made evident by the manifestation of speaking in tongues. Let me just say for the record that, that is hogwash! Speaking in tongues is only one gift among many. The manifestation of the power of God moving in your life is the evidence of the indwelling power of Jesus Christ in your life.

Some denominational practices will even go as far to tell you that if you cannot speak in tongues then you are not saved! Again – HOGWASH! From the moment that I told Jesus that I could not do this without Him, I knew beyond any doubt at all that I was "saved". There was no next step. I also know that Jesus himself told me I can set this down (meaning this life of commitment to him) at any time and walk away, of course the result of such decision separates me from the one I love. Why do you think it is important to preserver until the end? But this will set me off on a rabbit trail. That is a lesson for another day.

Back to the point. In a faith where we are to encourage and build one another up, why would you ever think it is okay to make a person think they are a lessor Christian because they did not have a specific gift? Furthermore, why would you try to steal away a man's salvation, convincing him or her that they were not saved because they did not display a certain gift? Shame on you! I thank God that I had the confidence of knowing who I was in Christ when I met these people. I saw the manifestations of Gods power flowing through me as a normal thing. Through this testimony I knew that I walked in the power of God. I didn't need some "heavenly language" to be who I was. Let's carry that logic out a bit here. What if I did not have the confidence and security produced by the manifestation of Gods power in my life? What if I "got saved" felt better, came to church and just saw my life begin to change for the good when someone of authority, like a Pastor, came to me and said that if I didn't speak in tongues I was not saved! It would shake my world! The foundation of my salvation would no longer rest on Jesus but on a "gift" I didn't understand. We may want to say that other people's opinions are of no importance, but in reality, it is hard if not downright impossible to walk through life secure in one's salvation when you are the only person

who believes you are saved. My salvation is
firmly held in place by Jesus Christ and him
alone. John the Baptist did not speak in
tongues, in fact there were no recorded miracles
by his hand. Was his salvation not there? Was
he less then another believer? Considering that
Jesus himself made the statement the there was
no greater among men then him, I am betting he
is securely in the presence of God today. What
about Stephen? What about the many men and
women throughout history where there is no
evidence that they spoke in tongues and yet they
have by record displayed many great miraculous
displays of Gods great power in their life? Are
they a lessor creature or worse yet lost to eternal
darkness? How dare you! To build a theology
around a single manifest gift is wrong. Our
theology must be built around Jesus Christ and
him alone. On the other extreme we have those
who teach that there are no miraculous powers
today, that that was only a b-12 shot if you will
for the church to get started. Then I would pose
this argument. Who has healed the many people
my hand touched and my lips prayed for? Who
made the prophetic word I released come true?
For that matter, who planted such a prediction
in my mind? Why would I know the

circumstances of a stranger's life and be able to speak healing into their wounds? Naïve brother, Is your god dead? Mine is not! The one true God is alive and powerful and he has given his people power so that the world, who lives in darkness may see his light and call out to him to be saved!

...Deep breath.... Calm down. Count to ten and relax.

The gift of speaking in tongues, what is it? I guess the best definition I ever heard was that it is a heavenly language, an unknown language among men. I really don't know the best definition. What I do know is through my personal experience. Before I share some of my experiences, allow me to point out that many people I hear speak in tongues make me wonder if theirs is a gift or a self-created gift. With a theology shared by some that your salvation depends on it or that your spiritual maturity depends on it that then it opens the door for a lot of good intentioned fraud and self-trickery. I will say this, based on my own personal experiences, I would wish for everyone to have this gift.

I had just gotten off of work and was driving down the highway on my way home. It was evening time and a beautiful evening it was. I saw a church up ahead, which is not an abnormal thing living in the Bible belt and all. This one in particular had a mess of cars in the parking lot. God spoke to me and told me to pull in there. So I did. I tried to unobtrusively slide in to one of the few spots open to sit down at. Apparently they were having a revival service and their service had already started. It was contemporary worship music. Hallelujah! Not that I have anything against gospel music at all. I actually like a lot of the old gospel music. There is a couple that I don't care for and a few that seem to focus on misery rather than the joy and the hope of the Lord, but outside of that, I really like gospel music. The problem I find is, churches that only let gospel music in tend to be very religious and formal usually at the cost of not allowing God to run the service. Now I am sure, well at least hope that is not always the case. However, for the most part, this has proven to be the case in my experience. Okay, let me pause for a moment before I dig my hole to deep. I have found basically three kinds of Christian churches. Graveyards that are so formal and religious that there seems to be no worship of the living God and you either conform or are an outcast. They are very religious and always have the feel of a dead place. On the other extreme we have what I refer to as a circus church. The people are running around operating in the gifts, or apparently doing so. Everything is chaos and there is very little to no order. In fact for a visitor, it can be downright scary. From the outside looking in it appears as though it is a mad house filled with crazies. The third type is somewhere in the middle. There is order yet liberty for God to do what God wants to do. There is leadership and direction however it is not a controlling oppressive leadership, nor is it minimal and without control. I have been in some of these "spirit-filled" services that have been off the charts. Thing is, they always seemed to have organization to them. As if they were choreographed. As in fact they were, only by God and not man.

...Anyway, I am getting sidetracked. Back to my experience.

I came into this church and took a seat on an end pew. I was observing what was going on and praying. I was scanning the crowd and listening for God to tell me why I was there. God pointed out a man sitting slightly behind me and across the aisle from me. God said to pray for this man and I began to. He told me what was going on in that man's life. It was a sexual addiction and the revelation from God was very specific about what was going on. Now, as a point of order, just because God tells me something about someone does not mean I need to tell them. If God directs me then I tell them. Otherwise it just means for me to simply pray for them. So I sat there praying for this man. When I finished, another man came straight up to the man I was praying for and began to pray for that man loudly, but in tongues. My first thought was, what a show off. I even said to God "listen to that man; it's a bunch of bologna!" That's when God retorted "Listen." I strained my ear to hear this man's words. Suddenly I could not only hear him speaking in tongues, but I also understood what he was saying. He was praying against the very same addictions and spiritual problems I had been praying about! WOW! This was crazy. That is when God told me that his spirit (the man's) was uttering words that his body could not express. It was the physical manifestation of a spiritual communication. I was blown away. Speaking in tongues was real. Some like to call it a prayer language, others a heavenly language, what-ever floats their boat. Point is it is real. I left that church that evening with a whole new perspective on this gift called tongues. After that I asked several people I knew how they received that gift. They shared their stories with me. Some were really wild and interesting. At this point I didn't speak in tongues. I did now know that it was a real gift and my prayer was that if it would make my ability to work in God's kingdom better, then I wanted it also.

Well it was on a weekend at a father-son campout with a church I loved. It was probably two in the morning. My son was asleep and I was sitting there praying and talking to God. Some of the other fathers and I had been up talking for a while and I had a lot to process. One of the things I had said to God was, again, I cannot help but feel like this speaking in tongues thing is something I need. Suddenly a strange feeling came over me and my mouth opened and this flood of seemingly non-sensical words flooded out. My mind was flooded with a wave of images. The images kept flooding in and it was as though my mouth was trying to describe this stream of imagery. It was crazy. I had not enough words in my vocabulary to describe the things I saw. It was pretty awesome if you ask me.

Today it flows naturally and it may take me weeks to unpack the information that is downloaded. I have noticed differences in the way things happen. In spiritual warfare it is very different from revelation, which is also different from healing. I am not going to attempt to teach on this controversial subject but I will tell you that it has become an indispensable tool in my intercession.

In Josh McDowell's book "The New Evidence That Demands a Verdict" he has an interesting passage that is very applicable here in regards to the spiritual gifts. He is not writing about such things but the logic and the wisdom still fit. He is actually quoting a man by the name of John W. Montgomery as he writes about the argument of Jesus resurrected.

"John W. Montgomery writes: "The fact of the resurrection cannot be discounted on a priori, philosophical grounds; miracles are impossible only if one so defines them-but such definition rules out proper historical investigation."

Basically he is saying that such things cannot happen if one makes a presupposition that dis-allows them. But that type of thinking is flawed in that it determines the outcome based on parameters set by opinion and not fact. Therefor it does not always make a true statement of fact. He exposes the argument that the resurrection could not be possible only if you dis-allowed it from the beginning of the argument. The reality is that if you allow the facts to speak for themselves you find that the resurrection did occur. It is the same argument with spiritual gifts. They are argued as not real only if you make a presupposition that they cannot be real. The fact is that while there is a mountain of fraud out there, there is a bigger mountain of evidence to the reality of spiritual gifts and miraculous power.

But again, this is not a book to convince you one way or another. It is a book to share with you my personal experiences on this fantastic journey with the God of creation. This book assumes you are already a believer and I try only to show you where I have walked in the hopes that it will cause you to move in greater places as a kingdom laborer of Jesus.

So if you found the last subject to be straining on your beliefs, then the next is sure to get your attention. Let's talk about spiritual warfare and the spirits that are a part of that.

I run into many Christians that will say that they believe in spiritual warfare, but if you begin to talk about demonic possession (or oppression as the case may be-please let us not split hairs here) they will tell you that it doesn't happen. Well except of course in primitive societies and places like Africa. If you talk about being under attack by Satan many will agree that it happens, unless of course you talk about physical manifestations of it. Yet for many, in the same breath, they will tell you about a ghost at Auntie Mary's house in which ashtrays are thrown about. I hear Christians talk about ghosts and the manifestations of them yet when it comes to things like a physical demonic attack or a demonic possession/oppression they will argue with you and tell you it is not real. Does anyone except me see that as a belief contradiction?

Many will try to explain away possession as an epileptic fit or some other kind of disorder. I have suffered from a mild form of epilepsy from birth; I also have a family with members with various levels of epilepsy. That doesn't mean we are possessed. Of course there are some who may want to argue that point! I say that in complete jest! The point is, if you have ever seen a case of demonic deliverance such as I have, you would see some very similar behaviors. At the same time you will see some very big differences.

I was in a country in Africa several years ago, yes Africa, when I got to experience some demonic deliverance. A young lady was having seizers and came to the church for help because the witch-doctors and the medical doctors could not help her. The medical doctors said that there was nothing wrong with her. The witch-doctors said that it was a curse put on her by a more powerful witch-doctor then themselves. Needless to say this woman had nowhere else to turn. She came to the village church because she was told that there was a man there who served Jesus and if he prayed for you, you would be healed. After the witch-doctors and medical doctors, she was skeptical but left with no other choice except to live with it, which was no real choice anyway. You see no man would take a woman like that for a wife because if it was medical he couldn't afford to care for her and she may pass it on to the children. If it was spiritual it may destroy his household. So she was not fit for a wife. She came forward in the church and as she was being prayed for she fell into a seizer like state. Her eyes rolled back in her head, she stiffened like a board, almost bit off her tongue at one point she even started to froth slightly at the mouth. Then something changed, she arched and began coughing violently like a cat with a hairball stuck in its throat. Next thing we knew a giant black slimy slug came out of her! My village pastor stepped on it and crushed it. After that she was obviously exhausted but in great spirits. She said she felt much better; that she knew it was gone. You could be skeptical, but two years later I checked on her and she was just married without ever having another seizer! A person may say whatever they want, but I know this woman, this Pastor, and these people.

In another place and time in Africa, I was speaking at a church when a woman suddenly went into convulsions. Instead of becoming stiff like a board, she became violent as she flung herself about. Thrashing here and there in the midst of our congregation, I ran quickly up to her and grabbed ahold of her. At the same time one woman grabbed her legs and tied them together, two others grabbed her arms and pinned her down. After about thirty minutes of aggressive prayer she started coughing and bam! She was better. She was a changed woman from that point on. Today, nearly a year and a half later, she is fine and without any more health issues like she had before.

Several years ago, right here in the good ole U.S.of A. I was with a group of people when a young lady came up to me and said "God told me you have what I need." Imagine my surprise. I said perhaps we should talk. We sat down and she began to share with me one wild story. She was born in another country in Central America. Her mother was a prostitute and her father a Vo-Doo witch-doctor. She was conceived and born with one purpose in mind; to be a sacrificial princess to Satan. She was to be, if you will, a bride of the devil. Her birth name reflected that very purpose. I will not tell you many details about her because you really don't need to know that. Anyway, there were a series of events and she was adopted into a good religious family. She shared with me how for as long as she could remember she had been visited by Satan every night. She was never afraid because to her it was normal. That sense of normalcy began to change when she was adopted by this Christian family. They held a senior leadership position in the church and therefore she spent a lot of time in church. There came a day when she gave her life to Christ. As a memorialization to this wonderful day, she wanted to get a new name; a good Christian name. She chooses a name she liked and that was her new name! Everybody in her adoptive family rejoiced. That night however, she is again visited, this time it was not Satan. This time she was terrified. This thing, instead of being beautiful and endearing to the eyes was hideous! As she lay in her bed, it stood at the corner of her bed and began to tell her something that haunted her for years. It introduced itself to her and said that it was here to remind her that she was Satan's Princess and she would never be anything else! Didn't she realize that? Even her new name meant princess. It would tell her to renounce this Jesus and come back to where she belonged.

She told me that she went and told her adoptive parents, but they believed that as a Christian now nothing of the sort could ever happen to her. They basically convinced her that it was all in her head. How sad. When I met her she had been dealing with this quietly by herself for years. Struggling alone and without relief from nightly visitations of a demon who mentally tortured her. She had nowhere to turn and no one to believe her. She was caught in a belief system that said what she was experiencing couldn't be real so she had to be crazy. To make it worse she began to feel as though God didn't even want her.

Now I really should have shared this story first because in all honesty, it happened well before any of my other experiences. You see, up to this point I only knew this stuff to be true because the Bible said so. Now I had met people that I knew spiritually there was something in them, something evil and wrong, but I never dealt with the intervention in their life before. So you can imagine my stupid look as the realization came to me that we had to do deliverance. More specifically, break the bond between her and this demonic association. To make all this worse, we were on a mission trip. So here we have it, we are both hundreds of miles from home living in emergency mission shelters surrounded by hundreds of Christians whose faith left no room for this kind of stuff. Yea me! My prayer was "God Help!" O wait did I mention that she was 17 and with her high school youth group. This past week had been the first time her group and I had ever met. I had worked with a few of the guys from her group that week and got to speak briefly to her whole group earlier that evening. This was definitely gonna be interesting.

I told her that I thought we should pray, but that her youth leader should be there also. So we got her leader and asked her to join us. I briefly explained to her leader that she was in need of some prayer and I felt it was appropriate for her to be a part of it. The three of us went around back of the dining hall where we would be away from the other thirty or so young people and the many other adults. I had no idea how to explain what was about to happen to the poor youth leader. She was a kind hearted woman in her late twenties or early thirties. She was raised up in her particular denomination and what was about to happen was so far out of her box, I couldn't even explain it to her. So I asked her to open us and begin the prayer. She prayed a very sincere concerned youth leader prayer. Something to the effect of God, you know what is wrong with so and so, please be with them and comfort them, may your will be done. In Jesus name, Amen. Then she was done. I took a deep breath, I knew what was about to happen, generally speaking because I read the book. I wasn't sure exactly what it would look like, but I was pretty sure that this youth leader was about to have her world rocked.

Picture this; it is dark, about nine thirty at night in a hot sticky June. The three of us are circled together standing up holding hands. We are in the forest behind a camp style dining hall. We have the whole reverence thing going on, the leader because she genuinely cares, the girl because she needs help, and me because I need God if I am gonna do what I know has to be done. The girl is quiet, the leader prays, now it is my turn. Many people will note that, more frequently at that time especially, I am not the quietest person when I pray. My insides are turning, I have never done this and I am not sure what to do. SO I took a breath and began. "Lord, you know what needs to happen here. You know that I don't really know how to say what needs to happen, but you know what needs to happen. Lord Jesus, I bring (girls name) and set her squarely before your throne." No sooner did I say that and she shrieked and went into some kind of seizer. Everything went wide open then. She hit the ground convulsing. The youth leader tried to hold her and had a bit of a panicked look on her face (or so it appeared to me). I stood with one had on the girl and a flood of words began to pour out of my mouth. Some in English and some in some kind of strange language I didn't recognize. I didn't speak in tongues at that time (or so I thought) so I had no idea what that was about. On the other hand we were in the midst of whatever this was that was going on and I was just rolling with what poured out of me. After several minutes, that felt like forever, something changed. It was like there was a noticeable difference in the air. The youth leader must have noticed it as well because she was now far more relaxed and holding the young girl in her arms as a mother would. The girl at this point was sobbing. I looked around, saw that I was done, saw that she needed comfort and that the youth leader could handle that so I left. As I came around the corner I ran into a whole mess of kids that were rushing towards us. They wanted to know what was going on, they said they heard squealing like an animal being killed. I told them it was nothing just praying with some people. I led them back into the dining hall and we played worship music and talked about the cool things they all saw God do that week.

The girl hugged me the nest morning before she went home telling me that was the first time she slept peacefully since she had been saved. She gave me a very special gift of a necklace with her name on it. It is one of my treasures along this fantastic journey with Jesus. I talk to her every now and then. About a year after that incident she told me that shortly after she got home her mother said that her father and she had noticed that there was a good change in her behavior lately. The girl said she got up the courage and told them what had happened on that trip. They apparently listened then explained to her that those things didn't happen, but they were glad she felt better. She told me she has never been visited by that demon since.

Those poor parents, bound up by the chains of religious presupposition.

I thank God for that young lady. I also thank Him for that experience, because shortly after I was about to find out how real and how deadly spiritual attacks could be. Up to this point I had heard many Christians talk about how the devil was attacking them. After this and a few other incidents close together I usually just smile and think; if you don't put gas in the car, you can't blame the devil when you run out.

Chapter 7

Digg'in in for the long haul

Something that we as believers tend to forget in practice is that we committed our lives to God's purpose and not our own. While we say that and affirm and reaffirm that in our religious ceremonies, in practice, we tend to not be as committed as we would like to be. I imagine it is because the perspective sacrifice appears to be too great. For example, one may think that their spouse would be upset about it or they may see it to be unfair to their children. Great purpose will require great sacrifice. Perhaps it will not require it all the time, but eventually there will have to be sacrifice to accomplish great things. Make no mistake about it, Kingdom work is great purpose! It is the greatest of all purposes.

You as a believer have purpose and potential in your life. Question is, do you want to see it realized? Are you willing to follow Jesus all the way to see it happen? Are you willing to bet everything in your life on the purpose of Jesus in your life? Understand, we all have purpose, yet our purposes are different from one another. Even to people called into the same kind of ministry, they have unique purpose in each of their lives. What is your purpose? I hear men and woman talk all the time about their calling and what they are called to do. I don't think most of them realize the distance they can go in that calling. "I'm called to be a Pastor" says one. Really? On the contrary, you are called to lead! How far will you lead the people in your charge? Another may say "I am a prayer warrior." Is that so, if you are willing to run the whole race in your calling, you may just find yourself effecting change in distant lands or stopping wars between countries! You see if we as believers would be willing to trust God and pursue our destiny in Him, you would see some become Mayors and Senators, and even Presidents. And it wouldn't stop there, if they could see the potential of who they could be and seize ahold of it and push into it, you would see Pauls' and Daniels, and Isaiah's, and Peters', and Moses's! They would be everywhere! The world around us would be a different place. Truly committed Christians would saturate every aspect of society. While not everyone is destined to become a Moses or an Esther, none are called to be a pew warmer. Many are not pew warmers for that matter, but we rarely step into our full potential in Christ.

It is in no way my purpose to make you feel guilty here, so I will try to be gentle in all I say in this section. Allow me to just throw out a few things I think of a lot. Did you ever wonder why you do not read anything about the children of the Apostles? I am not talking just about the Bible, but in historical writings in general. I think of the sacrificial life, relationally in a family, that many of the great men throughout New Testament history have made for the sake of the gospel message. I read Foxes Book of Martyr's and biographies of great laborers of Christ and see their sacrifices. I have friends who have been tortured for Christ's sake and they push on regardless of their wives and children. However, as a note in regards to their wives, I typically see that they swell with great pride because of their husbands' courage. But not always. I know men that stepped out in the courageous pursuit of the destiny God wants to give them only to be abandoned by their wife. Yet they took the sacrifice with great morning and continued onward. Kingdom courage is not stepping forward; it is stepping forward regardless of the sacrifice that will come along.

Look, I LOVE my son. I can't imagine not having him in my life and I never want to lose him. He and my daughter are two of the greatest treasures God ever placed into my life. Both children are treasured for different reasons. My daughter is my baby girl (even though she is now grown up) and she will always be my princess in my heart. My son however is a promise from God. God spoke to me about him before he was even born and before I even believed in the God who spoke to me! Shortly after my wife (his mother) left us, God said something that put a lot of things into perspective. My job took me over the road to make a food pantry delivery every Thursday afternoon. She knew this and she would frequently take him out of school and then make wild statements to me on the telephone about how I will never see him again. Usually she brought him home by Sunday, sometimes a day or two later. It was crazy as far as I was concerned. Thursdays became a dreaded day for me. There was nothing I could do and I would never know when this would happen. It was affecting his school and his behavior. It was tearing me up. One Thursday in particular I was crying out to God. "You gave me a responsibility to raise him up and I am trying the best I can Lord. You have to stop this, how am I supposed to raise him up to be who you created him to be if she keeps taking him out of my life? Look at her lifestyle Lord! She has gone far from you. Help me please!" If those were not my actual words they were pretty darn close! I still remember the weather that day, the sway of the truck going down the mountain, even the very spot this took place. Anyway, I gave my plea to God and suddenly He responded. It was not in an audible voice (I think), but it may as well have been. His response was so loud in my spirit that if anyone else was in the truck with me I am very sure they would have heard it also. God said "I don't need you to raise him up to be who I created him to be." Immediately, I realized that every day, every moment I get with my son is a privilege and a joy. Also, I realized at the same moment, God was right! He didn't need me to rise up my son; he was allowing me to raise him up! WOW! I cannot tell you how much pressure that took off of me. Not two minutes later my cell phone rang. It was her, she called to tell me she took him out of school and I would never see him again. That was the first time that ever happened that I was completely at peace. God had it under control. Neither a single day nor a single moment is guaranteed with my son. Since then there have been many short lessons like that. Continuations if you will of the first lesson. I realize that that doesn't truly represent a sacrifice at this point, especially when you consider that he is lying asleep on the couch as I write this. Of course today I face the renewed possibility that I will lose him. But I am strengthened to know, God has it under control so it will be okay. Actually I share this as a mild opening to the story of a couple mother's I truly admire and wonder how courageous I would be in similar circumstances. I pray I never have to find out.

The first is a mother who stood watching as the executioner stood poised with the axe over her child. Her son was seven years old and was sentenced to death for testifying to the truth of the one true God who set the stars in the heavens and gave life to all men. As the child wept the mother shouted from the crowed, "Don't you dare cry; today you will be in the arms of our Jesus!" With that, the axe was swung and the child was beheaded. This was somewhere in the neighborhood of 150AD.

The next was in about the 1970's. The father was already in prison, or perhaps dead, no one really knew at that point. He was there because he would not cease to share the hope of Jesus with the lost and unbelieving world they lived in. Instead of playing it safe and justifying her choices by hiding behind the needs of her innocent child, the mother too continued her husband's ministry of sharing the hope of Christ! Her reward? Prison! This left her 11 year old son to wander the streets of a brutal and intolerant country. He had to fend for himself and suffer the injustices of his circumstances.

In another example; the son to be executed unless his father renounced Jesus; the sons response – better I die and be with Jesus then live with a coward as a father. The mother who comforted her young children with words as she watched them one by one executed because she refused to renounce Jesus. History is littered with these stories. We like to believe that our God will swoop in in the last minute and save the day. Our children and our loved ones will not be lost and blessings will flow and all will be milk and honey from then on. Each of us in that situation would probably hope for an Abraham and Isaac moment. However those moments are far more rare then moments of great sacrifice. Sacrifice is the pavement of the road called kingdom labor. Jesus set the standard, how can we expect anything less than what our savior endured?

For the intercessor that chooses to dig in and go the whole way, your road also will be marked with sacrifice. I cannot tell you what your sacrifice will look like but it will be there. For some it may be great unceasing sacrifice until all seems lost. While for others it may look like little sacrifice. I cannot claim to know the mind of Christ in these matters, but I can say that each of us has a road to walk and the pavement of that road will be sacrifice.

I began to start understanding this as I began to intercede for a particular church and the birthing of what God desired to happen among those people. We tend to think of sacrifice as the giving up or letting go of something. However sacrifice may also be the enduring of something. In an effort to bring the gospel of truth to the gentiles, Paul and his traveling companions often endured difficult and hazardous conditions. By living on the sides of roads and in remote rural areas, they traveled great distances. Faced with hostile people and haunted by Jewish elitists bent on stopping the spread of the Gospel at all costs, Paul and his compatriots had their hands full. As you walk on the journey, you find that your life becomes a journey of endurance.

I began my intercession for this particular church with no thought of endurance involved. It was simply a matter of listening to what God wanted and praying it into existence. I got to learn the dangers and hazards early on. We talk about spiritual attacks, but who would have thought that they would come into my life as they did. I was lying in bed sound asleep. My wife was still with me in those days and she too was asleep next to me. It had been an amazing night of prayer at the church earlier that night and I was exhausted. I had been there praying with another man. I really don't remember what he was praying about there but he was engaged in some kind of warfare. I remember he was very animated, but I was in a battle at a different location in the sanctuary. I remember at one point sensing a force of darkness at the back corner of the sanctuary. I've not been much of

one for couth, so I took the easiest way to get to
where I needed to get to. I began running over
the tops of the pews. It was a fight and I was
geared up and ready to roll! I left relatively late
that night. It wasn't until this dark force finally
broke that I went home. I was beat. So there I
was sound asleep. I was violently awoken from a
dead sleep by the feeling of someone on top of
me and my heart being crushed from inside my
chest! I opened my eyes and could see nothing.
I could still feel the weight of something, or
someone on me. I could feel their knees dug into
my legs and their body weight on my lower
abdomen. After that first startling moment, I
realized what was going on and I wasted no time.
"In the name of Jesus I command you to go!" I
didn't shout, but I stated it as firmly as any
commander would issue a command to his
young troops. Immediately the pressure on my
heart ceased. The weight on my body was gone.
I am sure that many non-believers and sadly
enough many believers will try to explain that
event away with some kind of reasoning.
However, at the moment of my command from
the authority of Jesus, everything stopped.
There I was in my bed, no lingering effects, no
sense of darkness in the room. I got up and

went to my study where I praised God and wrote it in my journal. Then I went back to bed. The next night as I again lay asleep in my bed I was attacked again. This time it was different. It made the night before seem like a little "probing of the defenses" exercise by the enemy. Resting peacefully I all at once was woke up by a swift and focused attack. Although I will try to explain this point by point, you must understand that the attack was so rapid that it seemed to happen all at once. First, it was like a great spike was driven down in each of my legs on the bed. It pinned me and I couldn't move. Then a hand slapped over my mouth and nose so I couldn't breathe or yell out. Then it went for my heart again. It was crushing it. The pain was off the charts. My eyes were wide with surprise. I struggled under the force of its hand over my mouth, but no matter what I did I could not command it to leave. I knew right then that it wanted me dead. Suddenly, I was being drug down the hall-way into my living room. This had to be a dream, it couldn't be real. But everything felt so real. I couldn't see this thing that was attacking me with my eyes, but I could kind of make out what it looked like by the spirit. Even to this day, I've not been really happy that I

cannot see these things with my eyes, but I can
seem to perceive them with my spirit when I am
in battle. As I was drug down my hall way, into
the living room; I struggled to command it to
leave. Oddly enough, I wasn't in a panic. It
seemed to be just a part of what I was made for,
so it all seemed to flow naturally. That's when
the Holy Spirit spoke to me and said that this
demon has no authority to kill me. I suddenly
knew that all he could do was try to scare me,
and perhaps make it hurt a lot. Well news flash
for him, I was not afraid, however he was making
great headway in the pain department. This
hurt really bad. Not to mention, trying to find an
opening to get a breath into my air starved
lungs. They were on fire, my heart felt like it was
in a vice being cranked closed and it was gonna
pop any moment now. Where it had my legs
pinned it was burning. Calm seemed to settle
over me. Not the about to pass out floating into
unconsciousness calm. I've been there before
being choked out once or twice. No this was a
calming of my spirit. Suddenly I realized I did
not need to speak a command to this thing. I
simply shouted it in my brain. Immediately it
was gone. I could breathe. That was my first
thought. Praise God in Heaven, I could breathe

again. Ever stayed too long underwater. You know that moment when you cannot take a breath and you can see the surface. You know when your lungs burn and you just can't seem to get back to the top fast enough. That breath you suck in the moment you break free of the water. How good it feels. Ahhhh... That is where I was at that moment. This time there was lingering effects. I was really weak. My inner thighs burned badly, but there was no physical sign that anything had just happened. My heart seemed to be regaining itself, but I was so weak I could do little more than lay there. I finally got the strength up to sit up. I was in the middle of the living room. I was facing the hallway and looking straight down at my bed with a blanket drug half way off of it. This was no joke. This shook me up. This was something out of some kind of movie. It went against any logic in my brain. I just survived a massive spiritual attack and the only thing that kept me alive was this agent of the enemy did not have the authority to kill me. Had he had that authority, I was at his mercy and based on the sheer intensity of hate resonating from him, my goose was cooked.

Imagine what Paul felt like as he was pushed out over a small cliff, probably no more than four or five feet high and then pummeled with stones as big as your head until as some believe, he was killed. Even if he wasn't killed, he was left for dead, believed to be dead. After the brethren gathered around him and began to pray, think of the reality of his dangers he faced settling into his spirit.

We talk about spiritual warfare. We talk about our authority given to us from Jesus; the fact that the demons must flee when we command such a thing under the authority of Christ. But the harsh reality is, we should not rejoice at these things but rather rejoice that our names are written in the book of life! Because the fact of the matter is, they too work under authority, and if they are given the permission we would be dead, period. I think we talk about spiritual warfare and this battle that rages as if it were a movie or a video game. Beep! Only three lives remaining need to find an extra life so we can keep playing. This is real, and real people die. There are real repercussions for our actions. I don't know why Jesus allowed the enemy to come and attack me the way he did that night. I do know that throughout my walk with him everything has been a small step forward into a much greater place. An attack like that in the early days probably means much more vicious attacks latter on. It doesn't scare me; it is a part of my journey. If I would have thought too much of it in the beginning, I probably would have opted for door number two. But this is my walk; it is the walk I was created for. I will rejoice and walk it until I reach its end.

You see, it is part of enduring. If we set our eyes on the now, this moment or season of our life, then we will tend to get bogged down in whatever hardship we are going through. It is when we cast our eyes on the bigger picture, the end-game so to speak that we can preserver through our circumstances. This is the secret to effective intercession. Set your eyes on the bigger picture. If you do not do this, you will find yourself easily discouraged. You will become more and more frustrated and bogged down in a quagmire of ineffective prayer. For those of you who journey along the adventure of intercession, you will find that your scope of authority increases and so to, in all probability does the time in which it takes to see results.

Not because your prayers become less powerful or less effective, but because there becomes an increasing number of things that must be put into order for the promised outcome to occur. For example, there was a church that I was interceding for. God spoke to me about the place he wanted to take it. I had no doubt that God would deliver this church to its destination (I am speaking spiritually of course). I love getting to birth through prayer these things God wants to do. You know when, in scripture, in Genesis, it says that the Spirit of the Lord hovered over the face of the deep, or perhaps in your translation, it says something to the effect that He looked over the darkness; well that wasn't a casual look, nor was it a superficial stopping by. It is a brooding, much like a hen when she is brooding over an egg. Patiently laboring at it to bring about a desired effect. That is intercession at its best. You are brooding over Gods desire. Patiently laboring until its desired outcome. Craftsmanship of the highest quality. That doesn't mean you get to take credit for it, because you didn't actually do it. God did it, but like a young son or daughter getting to serve an apprenticeship with their father, we get to be a part of it. We get to be a part of crafting great designs in an elaborate tapestry of Gods making. I don't know about you, but for me, that is so super awesome. Like a carpenter crafting a very ornate treasure box, is the hands of the master craftsmen. I watch in awe as my father brings every design to life. He sands and cuts and nails. With great care and insight to how each cut must be placed so as to not be corrupted by the grain of the wood or the slip of the hand. To watch my heavenly father work inspires me and sends me to sleep with dreams of growing up and being like him.

With what He is crafting with this particular church, it amazes me. It started with a few small prayers like it usually does. God giving me a command, which always sounds more like a polite invitation than an order. In fact, I think it is a gross injustice towards God for me to say he gave me a command. My desire to please him and my love to learn from him causes me to run forward every time he offers. How many missed opportunities to be a part of Gods great plan do we have by getting distracted with what this world has. Those distractions are probably more deadly, at least to me, then frontal attacks like I described earlier. Frontal attacks are easy to deal with, put your boots on and fight. Real simple. These less obvious attacks are difficult. They are the snares the enemy lays down to capture you. They are nets to entangle you and pits to stop you. This journey with Jesus is a booby-trapped minefield. Observance and patience are the order of the day.

After stepping into this place of intercession over this particular church, I began to realize that it would be different then the churches I previously interceded for. A new game; which would make sense since the attacks were escalated. As usual I would begin my prayers by honoring God. Then I would search myself and repent of wrong things and places in my life. After that I would usually speak back to God the things or places or promises he has spoken to me concerning the place or person I was interceding for. In the beginning it is pretty simple; there just isn't much background to go over. Then I wait for God to direct me on what to do or pray. At this point, God began to speak to me about where he was taking this body of believers. As I listened, it just didn't make sense in my brain. I had gotten a chance to get to know these people a little bit and it just didn't add up. Surely God wasn't talking about these people. In fact there came a point when I even said, in reference to one person in particular "God have you seen him? Are we talking about the same person?" That's when God just said "Watch." It didn't take long, it was just several hours later and a fire was lite in that man and he was a different person. But the journey was just beginning. Typically at this point, my intercessory involvement would last only a couple weeks to a couple months. Little did I know, this time it would be years. Person by person, event by event, God would have me pray into each thing. At times nothing that was going on would resemble what God kept telling me it would look like. I would pray into it and worry over it. I would find that my heart would break over it and rejoice when victory would come. Sometimes my prayers would be defending from spiritual attacks against the people. At other times it would be a vision of what is to come up ahead on the journey and begin to prepare the people through prayer for it. I have been required to make an investment of myself into the people of that church. It has required a commitment on my part to labor in prayer even when I wanted to be done with them. One time in particular, I got so frustrated because they just didn't seem to get it, I threw my hands up and said "Lord, I am done with this, they don't care and they don't want it. I am leaving." I left them behind. Not another thought about them and I was fine. I was sitting in a church I go to from time to time in worship. It was amazing and beautiful. I was completely caught up in the worship. Dancing with Jesus. When out of the blue, he whispers to me, "I want you to start praying for those people again." There was not even a hint of condemnation or anger for me walking out on them. There was no, gonna give me the what for. Just a sweet whisper during a dance. I was there. I stepped right back in. I think I just needed a break, and Jesus let me have one. When I went back to interceding for them, my heart was renewed. My love for them grew even deeper. They are still on a journey and I am still on it with them. Nearly eight years ago God showed me in a vision who those people are and I have had the honor of seeing them step into it. They are not there yet and still have a journey ahead of them, but it has been amazing so far.

In the midst of this amazing journey I have gotten to taste the drink of loss and sacrifice. One can look back and see many reasons why my son's mother is no longer with me. What most do not know or understand is that her absence is a direct result of the enemies maneuvering. There was a time when she walked close to God. She was radiant in those days. We had been overseas together and fell in love with people from another land. She was active in a women's group and on a path to become a very strong prayer. It was in the early days of my intercession. As I was learning that it was going to require real commitment on my part. That's when the enemy struck. I was out of town and she fell right into his snare. Although I cannot tell you the exact circumstances, I do know the exact day and almost to the hour of the time. I watched her spiral into his camp. I felt completely helpless and labored away in prayer for her, but ultimately, one gets to make their own choices for their walk. Her and I can go round and round rehashing the "whose fault it was game"; arm-chair consoler's can present shoulda, woulda, coulda's. The reality is; Satan ambushed my family when I was unaware that these kinds of attacks really can and do occur. It took me several years of being caught in the endless trap of beating myself up thinking I should have seen it coming; I should have done something more; I should have.....   That in itself became a type of snare to me. Since then I have met several men who were faced with this same type of situation. Do I push forward with the kingdom work I have been given, or do I withdraw in the hopes that my sacrifice will be lessened. Is there really a choice? It is true that God told me years ago that I can give this up at any time, the truth is I can't. I do have that choice, but I am so in love with this Jesus that loves me. Like Peter said speaking for the twelve; where would I go if I were to leave you Lord?

Chapter 8

Grass on the road or grass on the hillside; which is greater?

For me being an intercessor has not been a simple; here is a task, get it done, check it off the to-do list. No, instead it has been filled with many interconnected tasks. In a county I still intercede for, I also intercede for particular churches that have significant roles within that county. These are my areas of direct authority. They are places I have spiritual command over. I am not the boss of anyone in particular, but spiritually, I have much authority and insight into the goings on in my area. As you mature as an intercessor, you begin to see your areas of authority. That doesn't mean that you cannot operate outside of your area of authority. It just means that that is where you function with real authority. At times you may intercede in a different area by invitation of a person who has intercessory authority or by Gods Holy Spirit.

In my job, I get to meet wonderful men and women and young people from all over the United States. At times, God has had me to intercede on their behalf. This is not a typical thing or is it something that happens all the time. But it is not out of the ordinary.

Sometimes God will have me labor in prayer for people I have never met before. For example, God had me laboring in prayer for several weeks for provision for a missionary in Germany. I knew his name and where he was. I had no idea what he did or what he needed specifically. Just "provision". Probably two years later, I was at a church visiting when in walks that man as a guest speaker for the church! Imagine my joy to put a face onto a man I got to labor in prayer for. I never had an opportunity to share that with him, but it would have been nice to talk about what happened from both of our perspectives.

I have stated previously that as a believer we are all intercessors to one degree or another. It is just a part of what we do as servants of the living God. We intercede into people's lives and situations on behalf of the Kingdom of God. Our intercession is spiritual through prayer, but also physical through meeting needs and lending aid. With that said, there is a place where some are called, or ordained, or perhaps they choose to go that way because it is a part of who they are created to be. That place is fierce kingdom building Intercession. Scripture says that God formed us and knew us from the beginning. He knit us together. It is more than just a physical assemblage of a person, especially considering the context it is used in. It has to do with every aspect of who you are. You have purpose, unique and original. Some embrace a unique purpose of intercession. Now I am not talking of the "everyday" intercession that we as transformed and redeemed followers of Jesus Christ are called to do. I am talking beyond that. This is prayer to the next level if you will. I use the word "embrace" because I am of the deepest conviction that every follower of Jesus has the ability to step into the highest levels of intercessory prayer. Take your "calling" as we like to say, and add to it passionate, godly, heartfelt, deepest sense of urgency and responsibility prayer, and you will see your calling soar to great heights. We make a difference, or we should be making that difference everywhere we move in our life. We as believers and lovers of Jesus should be making a kingdom impact in everyplace our lives cross with others. The Kingdom of God is within us. Well not everyone actually, just those who are redeemed by accepting Christ as their savior. Allow me to make an assumption at this point. I will assume that since you are reading this book you are passionate about your love for Jesus and living out that love. Based on that, I will tell you this, you are a kingdom person! Everyone from grandma who is praying unobtrusively for her grandchildren and anyone else in her realm to the global evangelist! Many times you will find that in the long haul, granny with her prayers make a bigger difference then the global evangelist. Not so much because either of them are better than the other, but because granny's prayers are usually deeply heartfelt and of earnest importance to her. This may be an exaggeration to some degree, but I think you get the point. Part of being a kingdom person, man or woman, is not just being in love with Jesus, but having his heart for the people and circumstances of this world. How do I express this? It is more than just knowing Jesus and doing what is right. It is doing what is right because godliness defines who you are. Remember, in the beginning God created man in His own image. Our nature was like Gods nature, only living in the fleshy shell God created for us to dwell in. Now when we are "saved" a restorative process is begun. For the most part we get to set the tempo or pace of that process. Basically, how far do you want to go in this fantastic journey? Our problem is letting go of the world and its hold so that we may run the distance. A lot of us exert our energies on learning the do's and don'ts of scripture but at the cost of failing to get too know the one that scripture is about. We get to know him, but usually at a lessor level than we are capable of. I encourage people to read the Bible over and over. Read it as a book in its entirety, than read entire books individually. Get to know the men and woman who wrote these books and those whom were written about. Get to know how they saw God, how they responded to Him and how He responded to them. This perspective is crucial to intercessory prayer. The success of your prayer life hinges on your relationship with God. It is not so much the voicing your opinions and cares on God; it is the listening for God to speak to you! If you don't believe God can speak to you than you are starting off in the wrong place. Now, I am not saying that He will thunder from the clouds (although that is truly not impossible). Read scripture, see all the ways God spoke to men, then understand, God is still the same. The only factor that has changed is us. We the believers have changed in our faith in what God can do. God is a constant. You want to see your prayer life explode? Grasp the concept that God can and does and will speak. Then LISTEN! I cannot stress that enough. LISTEN!

Good intercession, as with all good ministry, requires one to be "sensitive" to the Holy Spirit. For those of you who are familiar with that expression, you probably understand what that means. So bear with me as I try to define it for those less familiar with such an expression. When I first heard Christians say things like "the leading of the Holy Spirit"; "sensitive to the Holy Spirit"; and several other expressions Christians tend to use, I had no idea what they were saying. Did they have something going on that I didn't? Was there more to being a lover of Jesus than I knew about? It kind of makes you wonder about your faith. At least it did for me. Here is what I knew; God spoke to me. He told me what he wanted me to do, or say, or how to pray. This whole other stuff just seemed weird to me. Sometimes when we read the Old Testament we seem to think that every conversation with God had to be some kind of voice resonating from the skies above conversation. Maybe God manifesting in person and having a little meeting (okay, the pre-incarnate Jesus for you hair splitters). Imagine for a moment, God and Elijah sitting down and God laying out the plan for getting the people to come back to him. "Okay, you challenge the prophets of Baal, taunt them for a while, really get them riled up, then make a big deal setting up an alter for me. After that, I will take care of the rest. Wait until you see what I do here!"

Now I am very sure it didn't happen like that. Have you ever stopped to wonder and think on how God spoke or prompted these men and women to do the things that happened? What did they mean when they would say God spoke to them? These are worthy things to consider as a believer. When you read the Old Testament as I first did with no predetermination as to parameters for God or personal theology, it is fantastic. It is one of the most amazing journeys one could take. Through the eyes and experiences of men and women of old, God comes alive in history. I had no doubt God was real or alive; I had my own testimony to that fact. But to read other peoples testimonies and learn of even more amazing things than what I have experienced. It captivated me; it fed a growing fire, I wanted what they had! I wanted those types of experiences to be my kind of experiences! I was willing to give up everything for this fantastic God, this God who spoke to me and who called me from the darkness I had found myself trapped in; I wanted everything He wanted to give me! I still do. I want to see the mountains move, the tree uprooted. I want to see the dead raised, sick healed, blind with sight. However, more than these power flexing miracles, I wanted to experience birthing, creating, and loving. That was the true power. Now before you get going on some kind of "Mickeys got a power trip he is trying to capture from God"- thing. That's not it at all. We were created in the image of God. Think of the depth of creativity he has and exercises. The diversity that surrounds us. The simplicity yet complexity of all of creation. The foresight and attentiveness that God has for every detail. Take Jonah as an example. God created a large fish to swallow Jonah up, carry him safely, and spit him out at the correct place. The ground-work for that event was laid long before Jonah was even called from God to go to Nineveh. How marvelous!

Actually, I didn't realize how captivated I was by this fact until God pointed it out one day. Because I spend a considerable amount of time on the road, alone in a truck, I use it frequently to just talk with God. One day I was headed south with a truck load of food. I was rather animated as I tend to get from time to time as I talked with God. I was telling him that I wanted to experience those miracles that scripture says follow behind the believer as a testimony to Gods approval in their ministry. At this point in my walk I had been a part of several miracles. I had laid my hands on sick people who were healed, delivered possessed from the clutches of Satan. I have watched God take ordinary water and use it for divine healing. I had been a part of and seen many wild "God Things". But my heart desired so much more. I get wore out seeing so much hurt and pain and sorrow, I wanted God to use me in even more fantastic ways.

I was at a stop light when God, in that gentle and loving voice, spoke to me. He said "The things you ask about are small miracles. They are an interruption in a moment of time. They are like asking me to make grass grow on the blacktop road in front of you. Now look at that hillside. See the grass. That took more than a simple command. It took love and nurturing. It had to be planned and stewarded. Nursed and sung over. That is a greater miracle."

We take so much for granted in our life. Everything around us. Rarely are we amazed at the ordinary, like the grassy hill. Usually only when He makes the grass grow on the blacktop do we stand up and give him applause. But ALL creation testifies to his great might and authority. God wasn't calling me to be concerned about the immediate miracles; he wanted me to focus on the labored birthing and stewarding of his creation. That is really what intercession is. It is not the "Silver and Gold have I none, but what I do have I give to you, In the name of Jesus be healed!" moments. On the contrary, intercession is an investing of one's whole self into Gods desired outcome. You labor over it, you brood over it. You nurture it; sing your love song over it. You capture Gods vision of what it will look like and help to shape it into that end. You work side by side with your father and learn to be an excellent craftsman.

Please don't misunderstand me. It is not that healings, deliverances, provision, word of knowledge, and things such as that are not wonderful miracles. They are truly awesome displays of Gods deep resounding power. But to birth Gods will from the spiritual place into the physical place binds you to it. It requires you to invest yourself. You have a heart attachment to it that you cannot break. You have an emotional attachment to it that causes you to worry over it as a mother worries over her child. Immediate miracles are wonderful for the person they are happening to. Just ask the person healed from a life threatening illness or the person delivered from demonic possession. But to the one who prays over them they are nowhere near as fantastic in heart, memory, or testimony. On the other hand, for the one birthing Gods desire into reality, the intercessor, they are connected by heart, mind, and spirit to the event(s). In addition, the people involved in it experience all kinds of assorted miraculous moves of God in their life. Truly, the grass on the hillside is the greater miracle.

Chapter 9

The Big-Head people

When I was in the Marines I once had a lieutenant in charge of our company. He was a capable man, but there was an arrogance about him that made everyone despise him. He was what we called a mustang; he used to be enlisted, in his case I believe he made it to a lance corporal, which really isn't very high in rank at all. Then he went to officer candidate school and was commissioned a lieutenant. There is a distinct advantage in being a mustang. You are in a position to understand the struggles of your men better. However there is also the danger that you will think yourself better than your men because of your accomplishment. He fell into the latter of the two categories.   In addition to that, he held a Captains billet, his posting. As a company commander it was called for a Captain to be in charge. Because our battalion was shorthanded, a lieutenant got to fill the position. He didn't get his posting based on anything he did, but on the fact that we were shorthanded. Add these two things together and we had a real interesting time.   Now there is no doubt that he loved the Marine Corps. He wanted the best men, the finest company; he wanted Marines we all dreamed about. His problem, like many that did not labor their way to their place of authority is the size of their head. His arrogance and sense of self-importance cost him many good men of potential. He managed to alienate a lot of men. This resulted in the inability to shape a unit like he desired to lead. His own inflated self-worth prevented him from attaining (at least with that command) what he desired.

Have you ever worked with someone who got "that" promotion and they became intolerable to be around? Suddenly, they thought they knew everything. Everyone around them was an idiot, and all of the fault was with everyone else. They can never seem to attain what they desire because their inflated head is in the way! Maybe, you have even been that person. Hopefully, by now you have realized the error of your ways and corrected it. If not, may I suggest you put down this book and work on that.

Sometimes we even see that same behavior in a man or a woman that has worked very hard to get where they are at. They have attained their position by putting in the labor. Problem is they set a gulf between you and them, making themselves better then you. In reality they are not.

Many times I have seen a group of people come together to begin interceding for their church body or some other organization in which they also belong to. In the process of doing such an admirable work, they begin to be contaminated by the big head syndrome. Intercessors like this, ones organized into a small group but a part of a larger group, like a church, often fall victim to this. With wise attentive leadership this pitfall can be averted.

I have had the honor of working together with several skilled and capable intercessors. Even in these groups of people I have seen this terrible thing try to take root. Usually it begins when they try to become exclusionary. You hear things like "I don't feel like God wants that person to be here." Those are sure signs of a brewing big-head problem. Before you get to judgmental of the big-head people, understand that it is a part of human nature, the sinful nature, to do this. We as people with a sinful side to us, that dying man trying to live again, desire to be unique and important. We want to belong to that special group of people. We need to matter. In and of its self, these root drives are not wrong. Like most sinful tendencies, they are rooted in right desires, but wrong implementation. It is only when we bring those driving desires into alignment with the ways of God that we find that those desires will manifest into godly ways of life. Only in coming to the realization of who YOU are in Christ, and embracing that uniqueness, will you find contentment in who you are.

We each have different areas of authority and unique purposes in life. We will find that some of us have similar purposes, similar callings, even similar authority realms, but upon closer examination you will find differences between each of us. For example take two Pastors. They have the same calling, the same purpose, the same general aspects of spiritual authority. However they pastor two different groups of people on two different journeys before God. It's the same across the board. We are each unique. We are all the same before God, but we are also all unique.

I am going to focus on intercession for your local church that you belong to here. Bear with me and please try to carry these lessons over to other aspects of your intercessory life.

Many prayer groups form in churches all across the country. Sadly enough most of them never amount to much more than a group of good intentioned prayers. Usually they degrade into a gossip circle ending in a prayer for people. What a waste of great potential. I usually find that within these groups there is at least one person completely frustrated because they know there is more to this than what they experience in the group. They are usually passionate and have a sense of vision for the whole church. I love to see these people grow into who God created them to be. A pastor should always be looking for these people.

I am not really sure how to put some of these things down in an order that will really benefit you. Therefor I am just gonna roll with what comes out and we will go from there.

A Pastor and their churches leadership team should be involved with your prayer group. They should be there as often as possible, there should be a pastoral blessing over your prayer group, and there should be an open line of communication between the prayer group and the Pastor. Allow me to back up a moment. Let us set some boundaries here. Start with the Pastor and the leadership team in your church. Understandably there are many man-made rules in play in most churches. I will be speaking from a spiritual context, although it should be made manifest in the physical. That is something your church needs to work out. Perhaps you can begin to pray that into existence!

A Pastor is the leader of the church. I am so against congregational voting as the driving of a church; you cannot imagine. Think of Moses, can you imagine if he had to take a vote from the Israelites before doing anything? It is an unscriptural, man-made, devil inspired, destroyer of perfectly good churches. Voting has a place, but not in determining the path and journey of a church body. I am sure I just offended a whole boat-load of people, but such is life. I still love you and I do forgive you. You see the vote is a means for us, the followers to have control; it is rebellion, boxed up with a pretty bow so that we can feel good about ourselves. ....Since I'm on this subject, I will let it flow a little more. I think it is good and right for the people to vote for an incoming pastoral candidate. We, as a corporate body, need to set an undeniable point where we willfully and knowingly say in effect "We (your corporate body) recognize you, man of God to be a man who God has anointed to lead us in this time." You just gave the reigns of control over to that man. Submission would be the right word now, anything else is rebellion and that is not godly. With that said, he has a leadership team. These are his wise council. They help him to lead your people. But he is still the leader. The kingdom of God is all about order. We the people do NOT get to tell God how it will be done. Neither do we tell his representatives how it will be done.

Why is it important that I tell you these things? Simple, your prayer team is a part of the Pastors support network. You may remember that I made the statement before that you are on Gods side. This still holds true, but not at the cost of rebellion against Gods anointed. Remember how David had the man who killed Saul executed? That man dared to kill Gods anointed. Same deal here, we do not act as God in our station. We work as a part of a team designed to support God's kingdom desire for our church body. We lead in the places we are given to lead and submit in the places we are given to submit in.

Your Pastor is tasked with leading your corporate body into its journey before God. It is easiest to think of him as your own personal Moses, and your church as the Israelites. All of you are on a journey to your promised land from God. Your job as a prayer team is to help make that happen through intercessory prayer. As an intercessory prayer team, you will see many wonderful things happen. I like to equate it to Christmas. As a father, when I get my child something for Christmas I sometimes get more enjoyment out of it then my children. I get them that gift I know will really make them squeal with delight. I am so excited waiting for Christmas to get here so that they can open it. I stare at them expectantly as they take the gift and begin to unwrap it. My heart swells with joy when they get excited over that gift they have wanted all their life! It's like that as an intercessor. Often you will know what is coming before the people do. You pray it into existence and then delight when they receive it. You see the potential in people, the goodness that sometimes even they do not know is there. You watch them freed from bondage, launching into new lives. In my opinion, there is nothing more rewarding then effective intercession over a body of people. I am sure that as I journey along God will show me how I am wrong, and that is okay. I look forward to experiencing something even more rewarding.

This type of intercession requires one to learn what prophetic words are to be released and what not to release. You see, some are for the benefit of the group, so that their intercession may be more focused and effective. Some of these prophetic words need to be released to the Pastor and leadership team. And when I say released, I mean released! Let go of, you don't decide that he isn't moving fast enough and go release it to the congregation, or manipulate circumstances to be subversive and rebellious to God's anointed. If the Pastor is not doing with the word what you think he should be doing with it, than PRAY. Don't gossip, don't undermine your pastor, and don't beat his ears to death with your opinion. Just go to God, and let God deal with it. On behalf of Pastors everywhere, PLEASE listen to this.

There will be heart-wrenching times also in this type of intercession. You will see people's potential and at times watch them purposefully put distance between them and that potential. You will see people trapped in all kinds of bondage, but refuse to leave it. These difficult, heartbreaking parts are just as important as the good times. They are just as important as the times when you see God doing wondrous and miraculous works. It is in these times that our love is solidified over the people we are given to intercede for. You see our love is formed as we begin to see what God desires for this people. That continues as we begin to see the God potential in each of them. Wondrous things from God inflame that potential and give the people great encouragement to pursue God's heart for their people. It is the difficult times that solidify your love for your people. Patience and perseverance are what is called for here.

That is the general place for a church prayer group, an intercessory team. Now let's talk about some specifics. Only one can lead the group and you must have a leader. If you have no leader for the sake of hurting someone's feelings, than you will have a group that disintegrates and becomes unproductive. However leadership does not constitute a ruler or dictator, these too are counter-productive. A leader of such a group must realize that you are gathering the various resources of the prayer team and bringing them to bear. An intercessory prayer team is like a squad of commandos. Each of your people has a certain skill set. You target the objectives God gives the team with the appropriate skill set. You also have varying experience levels. Likewise you, as the leader must see and understand their experience. Teams and leaders and churches apply these strategies in differing forms. It usually takes a while to settle a team in with each other. I have had the privilege of working with many skilled intercessors. Sometimes they can be difficult to work with. Many are used to working alone in prayer and battle. Some are used to being a leader. They are usually very confident in their prayers and the way they think it needs to be done. Navigating the personalities of people can be a very precarious position.

Chapter 10

The Garden of Rest

In this chapter I am going to switch gears for a moment. It may seem as though this is unrelated to intercession, but really it is very relevant. Capture the heart of what I am about to share with you and you will truly see the perspective in which we must view our walk with Jesus. Our life is a life of intercession; both through prayer and by action.

I stood in a church praying over the building and congregation. There was a small group of people gathered there. It was their weekly prayer and intercession night. I was so pleased to be invited there to pray with them. I could not wait to see what God was going to do.

God gave me a destiny word to release to them. I released it to the Pastor first and he in turn allowed me to release it to his people. I may have been invited, but that in no way gave me permission to circumvent his authority. It was a wonderful time of prayer. It was a real time of encouragement and planning for that church body's future plans.

While I was in that time of prayer God had showed me something that I really wanted to reexamine. I knew there was great meaning in it so I could not wait until I returned to my room for some quiet time with just me and God. Upon our return I rushed in and got my evening duties completed as quickly as possible. I was chomping at the bit to spend time at the foot of the master. I knew tonight I was going to learn something great.

That is a part of intercession, well it should be a part of our Christian walk; spend real, intimate time with Jesus. Too many of us Christians are lazy in our relationship time with God. We pray and read and do all the perfunctory things required of faith, but left to ourselves, we tend to lose momentum and come to rest in our zeal for real time with Jesus. I find for myself that my zeal ebbs and flows, but at times there becomes not much ebbing or flowing. In those times I need a kick-start. But on this night, there was no kick-start needed. I was locked and loaded and ready to hear from the one I love.

I sat down and stilled myself. "Lord", I said, "I am here to learn from you." With that I closed my mouth and reflected on the garden he had showed me earlier. I had seen, by the spirit, walls and walk paths, and a bench. I had felt the sense of peace and contentment there. Not only did I long to return to this spiritual place, but I wanted to understand it. What did it mean? I patiently waited on God. Suddenly, without shock, but in such a gentle and immediate way, I was there. I could see the crystal like blocks that made up the walls. They were very tall. As you looked closely at them, examining them, they were smooth without markings to show how they were cut. The seams were so fine, almost imperceptible. They appeared to be finer than the breadth of a hair. The quality of the craftsmanship was astounding. I ran my hand over the stones. With only the most concentration that I could summon did my fingertips feel the joints. They were cool to the touch like quartz. They had the soft feel of quartz but the color of a dark aquamarine. I looked around and saw these walls that extended to a great height. Here where I stood, there was a bench beside me. Directly in front of the bench, but at some distance, was what appeared to be the front gate. I saw to my left, facing the wall, a great tower in the corner. It seemed to extend to a height of twice that of the wall. There were beautiful and lush flowers and vegetation everywhere. There was a path that glowed as if it were made from polished gold. They were like small bricks that were laid closely together. At one point they came to a walk bridge that overlooked a small stream. The stream glowed, the water seeming to have a brightness about it. It appeared to have a glow as if it alive as it flowed. It resonated with the color of a bright pearidote. It was not so bright as to hurt my eyes, it was pleasant. The walk path stretched onward with many hidden places. As I turned I could see that the path wound its way to the front gate. The doors of the gate were wide open. Inviting even. As though it was intentional that anyone could enter. I saw vaguely in outside the gate what appeared to be some kind of road. Suddenly, although I didn't experience it, I knew that when the Lords glory descended upon this place its walls would glow. A refreshed breath of life would overcome everything that was here. I suddenly realized that even the walls were alive. The logic in my brain couldn't make sense of that, but my heart knew it to be true. My attention was drawn over and over back to the tower. It was then that I heard the Lord. He said "Come up and look." I found myself immediately in the tower. There were openings all about its top. Like great arched glassless window openings. Then God spoke again, saying "What do you see?" I turned and looked to my left. I saw a sea of people standing off in the distance. They had shields and they were raised up as if defending themselves from falling arrows. However there were no arrows. I asked, "What is it that they are doing?" The Lord answered. "They are afraid of me so they raise up their shields to hide themselves from my love. They do not know me and think that I will be harsh and cruel to them." I asked the Lord, "What can I do?" He said go down and walk among them. Walk a little lower than them. Share my love with them. Reach up gently and touch their hearts. Their hearts will grow soft and they will begin to lower their shields. Then I will come and shower my love upon them as if it were a rain shower. Go walk among them.

Next, I turned to my right. There I saw a great sea. In the distance on that sea I saw an

Island. On that Island was a magnificent city. It was spectacular as it shown brilliantly in the distance. However I could see the back of the city. There I saw a brown vine growing up and over the city. In its newest reaches it seemed to cover the buildings. As I looked deeper into its growth I could see that it was destroying this magnificent city. I said to the Lord, "What is this I see?" He said this is his church. It was the city of the redeemed. The vine was destruction trying to consume this city and all who lived in it. It was complacency and religiosity. It was the tentacles of the enemy weaving his way in and among the believers bringing decay and destruction. I asked the Lord if I could go and take a bulldozer and just clear the vine root and all from the city. He said "No." He told me that within the vine are still saplings, tender shoots. If I were to bulldoze the vine I would destroy these tender shoots that can grow to become great trees. He said. "Go down among them and carefully clear the vine from around these shoots and nurture them and they will grow into mighty trees."

I turned again to my right and this is what I saw. I saw columns of people wondering through a dessert place. They seemed to be traveling aimlessly unseen by one another because of distance and dunes. They appeared to be weary and thirsty. I watched as one such column passed right beside an oasis. It had shade and water and fruit on its trees yet they walk passed it. There was a dune between them and this oasis. I asked of the Lord who were these people and why didn't they stop? He answered me and said, "They are on a journey to this garden of rest. It is a hard and long journey. They are weary and thirsty and are looking for a place of rest along their journey." "Why did they not stop at the oasis?" I asked. The Lord answered, "You look from a different perspective, and they cannot see what you see." "What can I do?" I then asked. "Go down among them," said the Lord. "Show them where these oases of rest are. Let them get strengthened and nourished on their arduous journey. Guide them to these places on their journey."

I then turned to my right again. I could see the gate of the garden. I could see the thick darkness in front of the gate and the short road that separated the two. I saw also a great beast that stood on the road. As people would come from the darkness on the road leading to the garden of rest, the great beast would ask for their toll. When they could pay none, the beast would throw them back into the darkness. I was outraged that this beast would stop people from entering into the garden of the Lord. In anger I cried "Who is this beast that he should do such a thing! He has no authority to stop people from entering your garden." The Lord answered me, "He has all authority to collect a toll, yet none can pay." "How then," I asked, "can these people enter into your garden? What shall I do?" Then the Lord gave me instruction. "Go down and walk among them. Carry your light low, for their eyes are used to the darkness. Do not hold your light high. Your light will hurt their eyes. It will frighten them and they will flee from you. Hold your light low. Those who desire to leave the darkness will come to you. Bring them into my garden." I then asked the Lord, "How will I pay the toll?" "You have no toll to pay," said the Lord. "You belong to the garden; there is no toll for you to enter. When they come to you, those that want to leave the darkness place your arm around them and walk them to the garden. The beast will flee to the side of the road and you will pass unharmed."

Some may say that this was something conjured by an over active imagination. Yet it was not. It was a vision yes, but it was so real I wonder if I was not some-how transported there. Every one of my senses were alive. I could see, hear, feel, and smell. When this experience was over I sat in my chair exhausted as if just returning from a long journey. Regardless of how I should define this beautiful experience, of which I refer to as a lesson from the foot of the master, its teachings are so dead on. It accurately describes the four basic types of people in life. It also presents the right way of dealing with each kind of person, or people group. To begin with we go and walk among them. That is intercession. First, we have to see spiritually who the person is, the situation they are in. We have to have kingdom vision. What does God want to accomplish in this. How should I proceed according to kingdom perspective? Basically, we, as intercessors, allow God to show us what is really going on. Then we say, "What should I do?" After that we do what God said for us to do. When we intercede, we do not have the liberty or right to impose our desire into a person's life. We are working on behalf of the King of kings. Therefore, we intercede on His behalf.

Sadly enough people will often fail to do what we so clearly see for them to do. One of the heart-breaking elements of intercession is this very fact. You, as an intercessor, will often see plainly what they cannot see. You could tell them but their tendency will, to at best, pay you a placating yes and go on and do it in some other direction. This can build a much calloused heart for the very people you need to love. You see short term intercession can be relatively easy by comparison. You're in, you pray, you're out; end of party. But invested, prolonged intercession requires something much more. It requires an investment of your heart, your being. You will have to love not just what you do, but who you intercede for. They will have to become a treasure to your heart. Like a father or mother looks at a child, so you will have to look at the person or persons you are interceding for. You birth destiny into a situation, into people's lives. This isn't the on the spot miracle, this is the brooding over investing miracle. It is the greater miracle. This type of investment will require something great from you and that is forgiveness. When they disappoint you, perhaps even doubt you or shun you. Your task is still there and forgiveness must come forward. It must come quickly and without hesitation. But it must also be correct forgiveness. Therefore we will talk about the right foundation of forgiveness. The relationship between forgiveness and love.

As a follower of Jesus Christ, forgiveness is of the utmost importance in our life. Our Lord tells us that in that same measure we apply it, so to shall it be applied to us. Nothing breaks my heart more for a fellow believer than to hear them say "I just cannot forgive them." Forgiveness is paramount in our lives. We forgive because Christ first forgave us. As a man or woman being crafted into his likeness, forgiveness no longer becomes a nice thing or a good thing for us to do; instead, it becomes a mandated character trait of the professing believer in Jesus. To be a professing believer in Jesus Christ and not have forgiveness as a foundational quality of our thoughts and of our heart, is to be no more than a wax replica of a baking pan. Your Christianity will be unable to bear up in the fires of life. Unlike prophecy, words of knowledge, miraculous outpourings of healing and resurrection; abilities to perceive the shadowy world of spirits both demonic and angelic; forgiveness is not a tool to be unholstered when it is convenient. Forgiveness is a quality not a tool. It is a part of the believers hardwiring.

All of us, if you go to church long enough will hear a sermon on forgiveness and its importance. Many of these teachings and sermons will try to encourage you to forgive those who have hurt you. Usually with this line of thinking: *Forgiveness is for you. The person who hurt you is not losing any sleep over the hurt they inflicted on you. Forgiveness allows you to move forward and not be imprisoned.* A cry rises up from the pulpit that says "Forgive those who hurt you so that you may be free to go forward in Christ's will for you!" For those skilled orators, this results in a flood of believers running to the alter, seeking the freedom of these chains of imprisonment. Cries of repentance waft heavenward like the incense burnt on the sacrificial alters of old. Tears freely flow as well-meaning brethren minister among one another. Joyous songs of worship are lifted from the lips of the children of God. Great relief settles among so many in suffering as we conclude our service and head in our respective directions.

Sadly to say, forgiveness built on this platform is selfish. It is a self-serving, self-gain, self-orientated forgiveness. Do we really believe that our Lord, the Glorious one of heaven, the King of kings, forgave us so that he could feel better about himself? Right forgiveness does not rest securely on a foundation of self. NO! It rests securely only on a foundation of love. We forgive because we love. We love because we know in that person, beyond their offense, is a person created in the likeness of our beloved one. We forgive because Christ forgave. To not forgive is to set ourselves in Christ's place of judgment, and if we judge, than we leave Christ only with the same standard we used. Therefore we condemn our self. If we forgive, but our forgiveness rests in selfishness, than we have not forgiven at all. No, we have made our selves feel good. We have deluded our self into proclaiming our own sense of godliness. No longer do we wear the robe of Jesus's righteousness, but we dawn a robe of our own righteousness. Which is no righteousness at all; rather it is a cheap imitation.

The forgiveness of Christ was established not on self, but on love. For He who was at the beginning, who gave life to all. Him, who established the foundations of creation, saw fit to love his creation. Because of his love he removed himself from his rightful place in the highest levels of the heavenlies and became like that which he created. Furthermore, because of his great love, he became the scape-goat of our transgressions as if they were his own, so that we, the transgressor, may be restored to God. Forgiveness made manifest through action.

When we, as the follower of Jesus, follow his example, it must not just be the action, but also the motive. We forgive, not because it makes me feel better. Not because it sets me free from bondage. We forgive because it is our nature. How is it our nature, when our nature cries out for unforgiveness? Because I am not talking about your former nature, but about the nature of Christ which lives in you now. As such, in that nature of Christ which lives in you, you forgive because you love them. You suffer their words and their hostilities. You endure with patience their insults and all forms of injury. You do this because you see in them something they themselves do not yet see. You see who they were created to be. A son or daughter of the one true living God. You see them as your relation waiting to be born into the kingdom. You see in them the potential that God spoke into them from the beginning. You see in them what God saw in you; someone of value and worth. Someone who has purpose and destiny. In their arrogance they live in ignorance. They do not know what it is they do. They are like a small child behaving badly. One whom we might scold but not out of hate and outrage, rather out of love. They do not know any better. Their eyes are blind and their ears cannot hear. They are like the idols they serve. There is no love in them because the one who is love is not in them. But they are not our enemy. For it is that very person we are dispatched to bring into the light. How can we bring them into the light if we, who can hear and see and love, bring them only darkness. Forgiveness is not self. However true forgiveness will bring you freedom and peace. More than that, true forgiveness will illuminate the darkness of the world. It stands as an

undeniable testimony to the love of Christ. True
forgiveness is unmovable and unyielding as it is
assaulted by the schemes of the dark one. It is
undeniable against argument. True forgiveness
releases all claim to self, all justification and
vindication for offense. It releases from bondage
not just the one who forgives, but also the
transgressor. True forgiveness is not offense
stored away as a delinquent note, to be retrieved
and placed in the balance of the scale. On the
contrary, true forgiveness is the debt note
burned without remittance of payment made to
the one who is owed. It is transgressions
forgotten. Not in the context of being erased
from ones memory, but in the context of not
brought forward in argument again. No longer to
be an obstacle in relationship; not with you, not
with God, nor with any other man. The
forgiveness of ones transgression against the
lover of Jesus becomes a bond of greater love for
the transgressor. An investment if you will, into
the potential of who the transgressor should
become when that joyful moment might come
when they themselves become a part of the
bride. It is a part of the long suffering of the true
believer. Not to be mourned and looked upon
with disdain. The opportunities of forgiveness

are to be cherished as moments to be crafted more into the likeness of the one we love. Right forgiveness cannot be given out sparingly or begrudgingly. It must be quickly surrendered. Lavishly poured out. Never to be removed and filled with the true heart of Christ. To walk in true forgiveness is to walk in love, and to walk in love is to walk in the ways of Christ.

An intercessor must walk upon the right foundations of the ways of Christ. An intercessor must walk in the ways of Christ. For we birth what was spiritual into what will be physical. While we do not make it happen, for God does that, He allows us to be the son or daughter working side by side with the master as he crafts his masterpiece. We use his ways and his tools to craft with. Every stroke of the brush applied to the canvas creates what is from his heart. He allows us to brush on his canvas under his direction so that when we are finished, the most magnificent of all brides shall be prepared. She will be a fitting gift for the King of kings. It is a gift that could never be prepared by our own hands without his direction. It is a gift for our father that we are unable to attain for ourselves. It is his heart's desire of which we could never purchase, yet out of love, he embraces us and shows us the way. It is perhaps the most honored place one can have: To work at the side of the master craftsmen on the labor of a master tapestry.

Chapter 11

To sum it up

As I stated in the beginning, I really do not think this would make a good text book. I did not write it to be a formal study guide. I did write this to share with you some of my adventures in intercession on this wonderful journey with Jesus. I hope you have found it encouraging and even entertaining. However, before we end our time together, I would like to take an opportunity to recap on some points that I think are important to walk away with after reading this book.

Remember, we are all intercessors to one degree or another. Intercession is by definition, the act of interposing oneself into a situation on behalf of another. We act as agents of the living God. We call Jesus our King. When we really mean this, we must remember that it is the submission to this fact that defines the parameters of our authority. We do not have the right to make any representation of Jesus outside of His nature. More than that, we have no authority to make representations outside of his goals and desires for his kingdom. Our knowledge of our Kings desires and kingdom goals come from more than just getting to know his written word. It comes from a personal and intimate relationship with him. Asking him and listening for his answer. Building relationship with him and allowing him to build a deep relationship with us. Remember, Jesus wants to reveal himself to us and through us. We, as his followers, his subjects are the true testimony of his awesome redemption. Out of love and of his own purpose, he chooses to use this living organism we call the church to truly convey his message of love and hope to the world. When Paul writes/quotes scripture and says that we are to come out from them and be separate; it means far more than in identifying name only. It means having our character and nature accurately portraying his character and nature.

The nature of intercession requires us to empathize with other people. We get to "feel" what they "feel" often. Sometimes we get to stand in a really wonderful place and get a glimpse of Gods heart for a people or situation. Although both of these situations can be overwhelming at times and even completely heart-breaking; it is something we as an intercessor should rejoice in. It is moments like this that draw us closer to God and help us to fall more in love with Jesus.

Walking in the place of organized group intercession will open us up to a variety of spiritual gifts and their operation. Because of this we as intercessors find ourselves subject to the pitfalls of a frequently used stratagem of Satan. Pride and an inflated sense of self-importance are some of the results of this snare. I like to refer to this as the "big head syndrome". Usually it manifests itself in the form of exclusionary club mentalities. People begin to think that this person or that person shouldn't be involved in the intercessory group. Although it is usually well intentioned, we must be very careful to recognize when we are stepping into the traps set by Satan. Remember, the thing we tend to forget about being deceived is that the deceived doesn't know they are being deceived. When we know we are being deceived and continue to walk in that path; we are no longer deceived but in rebellion.

I have found, and please understand that this is just a practice I have found to be effective. I imagine there are other practices that may be just as effective. When you are starting an intercessory group; start small and by a Holy Spirit led invitation for your beginning group. This establishes your group with a team of God chosen intercessors. After your group has begun and established itself, you may want to open it up to your whole church through a church announced invitation. Maybe you would want to play it low key and just have an open door for anyone who expresses an interest. Remember, there are many graduations along our walk as a believer. Some people know that they are called by God to be an intercessor. Some may just be interested in learning about intercession. For them, they will find that it is either something they are comfortable with or they won't. Either way it is an experience that should profit them. Others will have no idea at all; they are just looking for a place to fit in and be a part of something great; something bigger than themselves. Keep your door open. Encourage people to be active in function and learning in their intercession. While it is true that there will occasionally be wolves dressed as sheep who come to destroy what is being done in your intercessory group; it should never be used as a justification to bar group participation. Typically these agents of the enemy are deceived and have no idea that they are being used as a saboteur. They really cool thing about God in this situation is that if you allow the person to participate in your group when they desire to; they will sooner or later (usually sooner) have the deception lifted. With godly group leadership you thwart the ambitions of the enemy and use his plot for the growth of the kingdom. On those rare occasions when the agent is fully aware of whom they are and what they mean to do, you need not fear for God will not abide this predator for long. He or she will soon be exposed for what they are. That is the really cool thing about a group operation within the boundaries of godliness; you do not need to sweat these small things.

Intercessors are frontline combatants. They wrestle with things spiritual and physical. However they utilize the nature and character of Christ for their arsenal. They are a people who must always be considerate of long term implications to their actions. As an intercessor you are granted knowledge of a much larger picture to things. This knowledge sets upon you with great responsibility. It is something that must be taken seriously. In addition to that, it requires submission. To circumvent the God established order of things is counterproductive to our task. It harms the very people and situations we are called to intercede for. It opens us up to avenues of destruction from the enemy. We place ourselves in harm's way. These battles we are involved in are difficult enough without setting ourselves up for failure.

Another place intercessors tend to find themselves out on a limb in is when they operate outside of their areas of authority. When you do this you find that you are operating under your own power and that exposes you to vicious attacks of the enemy. These types of attacks can do terrible damage to you and the people around you. A good intercessor knows and understands their boundaries of authority. Sadly enough, many intercessors do not walk completely in their areas of authority. This lack of consuming the fullness of your realm of authority prevents you from being as effective as you could be. Again, a good intercessor knows and understands the boundaries of their authority. The revelation of these boundaries comes from that intimate relationship with Jesus. Our King is the one who assigns our boundaries. When you are operating alone or in a group, it is imperative that you know your boundaries. When you lead a group, often that group will operate under your boundaries. Therefor it is that group leader's responsibility to know fully where it is safe for that group to operate. You do not want your intercessors to be in harm's way any more than they must. Remember, this can be dangerous work. After all it is a war we are fighting. Chaos tends to be unleashed in the lives of competent intercessors. By operating within the right boundaries, you have the right protection: Gods. When you are in the right place, the enemy has only that authority God has given him to have in your life. You exceed your boundaries and then the rules of engagement for the enemy changes. At the same time the power of your intercession and your ability to defend yourself are greatly reduced.

Remember your perspective. We live by a kingdom perspective. When we look at people and situations we do not have the luxury of seeing them with worldly eyes. Think of the Garden of Rest the Lord showed me and I shared in this book. Our ultimate goal when dealing with people, weather "saved" or "unsaved" is to help usher them into the presence of the Lord. It is in that place that they can find their hearts desire. When we stand looking from this vantage point, as I stood in the tower, we have to remember that we see things differently than they do. Therefor we need to exercise a much greater level of patience with them. We have to remember that to lead these people or person into the place God is calling for us to lead them in, may require us to stand quietly and prayerfully by. We can't force them into that place. Neither can we manipulate them into it. They must be loved into it: Which is why we must love them! Only when we truly love them are our hearts positioned to release deep heart-felt prayers on their behalf. This combined with an understanding of how God wants to deal with the situation makes for an atom bomb of prayer.

One might say that intercession is a ministry where spiritual gifts are tools. Intercession by prayer or other ministry fields is kind of like an occupation. The spiritual gifts God provides for us are tools used to make our occupation more effective. Embracing the gifts of God is important. Believing in them by faith is important. Exercising them often is important.

Implementing them effectively and correctly is just as important. Don't abuse the gifts God gives us to use; it just brings harm to people and even yourself. Don't exercise your gifts outside the parameters of godly authority; that too brings harm. Don't abuse your gift; that brings destruction. Don't treat a brother or sister as less because of their gifts or lack of them. To do that can bring death to their walk. As ambassadors of Christ, we are a people who bring life.

Keep in mind that effective prayer does not come from incantations. The words we speak are not magic words. Instead they are an expression of our heart. The power of our prayer does not come from the copying of someone else's effective prayer. It comes from that intimate relationship with Jesus. As our heart falls in line with his heart it is than we can see powerful results. On this note remember that "In the name of Jesus" affixed to something doesn't give it an extra boost of power. Jesus is the only name given to us by heaven in which there is power, but it is because of who he is and not what he is named. It is not that it is wrong to say "In the name of Jesus." That's not it at all. Utter this beautiful name because it is true not to make it true.

Last but not least of all; forgive and love. Do both of these lavishly. Do not withhold either. Find your joy in loving people and forgiving people. Be quick about it and never be slow about it. Be a blessing to everyone. Let the world see the love of Christ pouring through you. Let your countenance glow having that fragrant aroma of Jesus wafting about you. Dance with the creator of all things. Be expressive to him in all your worship; in song and dance and labor and relationships.

May God Bless Each of You!

Other Resources at

The Most Excellent Way takes you on my personal journey. It starts in my youth filled with potential and travels into a place of worthlessness. In the midst of my despair hope shows up unexpectedly. Many people travel down very dark roads, some darker than mine. No matter how dark your road is, Jesus loves you and sees worth and value in you.

www.mickeywilcox.org

The Most Excellent Way

A journey from life to death, to the life of everlasting hope.

For some, the road we walk can become dark and hopeless. All bridges of retreat are burnt, all worth stripped away. But there is one who will rescue you, because he loves you. This is my journey.

Mickey Wilcox

Paperback $11.99

Videos:

Documentaries

Africa Vision 2011..............88min......................$5.00

Pakistan 2012...................35min......................$5.00

"12 Minutes With Mickey" Bible based teachings

Each DVD will have 3 teachings of your choice. $4.00 per DVD

Titles

Christian Life   Are you just a 10% Christian   Let's get Serious   A Different Kind of people

Unity Among the Body pt1   Unity Among the Body pt2   Unity Among the Body pt3   Unity Among the Body pt4

War   Islam as a Christ Follower   Petting your Sin
Positioning for the Blessing pt1

Position for the Blessing pt2   Position for the Blessing pt3
Position for the Blessing pt4

Thoughts on Forgiveness   What sin is Too Much
Isaiah 58   Unity of the Body

Relational Prayer   Living Stones
Church Love   A Fathers Love

The Beatitudes (9 part series)   A Nobel Task   As We
Have Opportunity   In Christ Alone

Practice Makes Perfect   Stephen   The Most
Excellent Way   Psalm 34 pt1

Psalm 34 pt2   Peace   Who We Are
pt1   Who We Are pt2

Daniel   Alter and Monuments   Stops Along our
Journey   Intercessory prayer 101

Choosing to Let the Light Shine   Opportunity to Glorify God
Foundation of Love   Sing Your Song

Footsteps   Semper Fi
Perspective   Hidden Sin

Fruit of the Spirit   Be Separate   Sin is
Crouching   Weathering the Storm

1st Peter 3   A Friend and Restoration   A Look Back at
Matthew 5   A Reflection on 1 Cor 13

As Sheep Among the Wolves   Be Safe   Blood on our
Hands   Cain and Able Offerings

Fellowship and Grievous Sin   How Can You be Glorified God
Love Your Enemy   Patient Love

Provision of God   Psalm 119   Quality and
Quantity   Reconciliation

Relationship With God   The Way of Love

Requests for DVD's and Books can be emailed to: usmc_mic@hotmail.com

Learn more about the exciting ministry I am involved in at **www.mickeywilcox.org**

For questions, speaking engagement schedule, or to learn more about this exciting man named Jesus; email me at:

usmc_mic@hotmail.com

www.ingramcontent.com/pod-product-compliance
Lightning Source LLC
Chambersburg PA
CBHW060239050426
42448CB00009B/1506